KNOWING RIGHTS

For all the Oberweis kin and Matt Petrocelli
And for Birgit and Micah Musheno

Knowing Rights

State actors' stories of power, identity and morality

TRISH OBERWEIS
American Justice Institute, USA

MICHAEL MUSHENO
Arizona State University, USA

Routledge
Taylor & Francis Group

LONDON AND NEW YORK

First published 2001 by Darthmouth Publishing Company and Ashgate Publishing

Reissued 2018 by Routledge
2 Park Square, Milton Park, Abingdon, Oxon OX14 4RN
711 Third Avenue, New York, NY 10017, USA

Routledge is an imprint of the Taylor & Francis Group, an informa business

Publisher's Note
The publisher has gone to great lengths to ensure the quality of this reprint but points out that some imperfections in the original copies may be apparent.

Disclaimer
The publisher has made every effort to trace copyright holders and welcomes correspondence from those they have been unable to contact.

A Library of Congress record exists under LC control number: 2001022165

ISBN 13: 978-1-138-72277-4 (hbk)
ISBN 13: 978-1-138-72276-7 (pbk)
ISBN 13: 978-1-315-19341-0 (ebk)

Contents

Acknowledgments

The authors would like to thank Steven Maynard-Moody, Marisa Kelly and Suzanne Leland for their efforts in many stages of this research, including the design, data collection and the many conversations that helped us to focus and refine our work. We would also like to thank Peg Bortner, Angela Trethewey and Austin Sarat for their helpful feedback on earlier drafts of this text. The authors also wish to thank Elizabeth Mertz, Steve Herbert, Dennis Palumbo, David Goldberg, Susan Coutin and Claire Annals.

Trish Oberweis also wishes to thank her husband, Matt Petrocelli, for his single-handed ability to make her laugh and for his going the extra mile to support the project. Michael Musheno thanks Birgit, his spouse, who thinks with the best of them, and Micah, his daughter, who made sure each family member had a fair share of time of the home computer.

1 Power, Identity and the Right to be Right

People act from the grounds of multiple and interconnected identities (see Butler, 1992) and reveal fluid, fragile selves (see Aronowitz, 1995; Butler, 1990; Mouffe, 1995). State actors, too, act from the terrain of identity. The link between action and identity has particular meaning for individuals who assume identities as state agents.[1] Law and policy are ultimately implemented in the daily decisions made by street-level state actors: law in practice is finalized at the ground level (Lipsky, 1980). Ultimately, it is these street-level workers' privilege and duty – it is their right, within certain constraints – to decide what is 'right' for any given case. Law, as the codification and communication of formal rules, is a weak guide at these discretionary moments. Instead, it is in these moments that workers constitute law by authoritatively asserting improvised norms and nuanced valuations of people and circumstances. This book explores the combination of identity and moral orientation as they affect the valuations of people and circumstances and at the level of defining those circumstances. Understandings of what ought to be are shaped not only by the rules, but also by the moral views of state agents acting on the identities of citizens, giving law meaning in the context of those discretionary moments.

Michel Foucault situates the police at a point of origin in the formulation of the modern state. ' "The police" appear as an administration heading the state together with the judiciary, the army, and the exchequer' (Foucault, 1988: 155). In this position, the traditional role of the police 'was to foster civil respect and public morality' (ibid.:154). It is this administrative definition, one that positions the police among the managerial politic of the state, that this study takes up, examining the administration of identity and good citizenship and also the administration of state goods and services.

In modern America, state administration is undertaken by a myriad of highly specialized agencies. The police are only one of these agencies and administer the state most obviously through negative forces, but clearly police have a positive, creative (productive) effect on citizens as well. Police officers

1

often characterize themselves as, and are often perceived by other citizens to be, more upstanding, and therefore able to protect 'the moral' (see Herbert, 1997).[2] Part of the discursive constitution of the identity 'police officer' is the shared assumption (by officers and by many other citizens) that they are the 'good guys' (Reuss-Ianni, 1983:1).

Another present-day agency administering the state's goods and services focuses on the task of returning citizens living with various disabilities to the workforce. In vocational rehabilitation agencies, counselors wield state power and act as agents of control as they allocate state resources to particular clients, fulfilling an administrative component of state power that Foucault clearly addresses.

We examine stories told by workers from each of these two state agencies for their combination of identity and moral content. Our analysis suggests that identity and moral views are intertwined and that together they partially drive the decisions made by state actors, changing the homogeneity of 'state morality' into an array of subject-bound moralities working through, within, around, or at times even in contradiction to state law and policy. The apparently homogeneous 'state,' in practice, is comprised of diverse representatives, each acting and making decisions at the moment based in part on individual identities, moral views and experiences.

Michel Foucault suggests that power, right and truth form a triangle (1980: 93). Where there is power, there is the right to determine what is true. The three come as a set. Moreover, the triad holds when 'right' is taken in either of two ways, first as a set of freedoms, as in 'a right to' do something (or not) and also in its moral, normative sense, as contrasted to what is 'wrong.' Both of these senses are important in placing the state and state actors within this triangle of power, right and truth. This is the sense in which we want to bring a notion of 'right' to bear on state agents' discretionary decisions, as a double entendre which fuses truth with power.

State agents' individualized interpretations of the legal order (and the actions driven by such interpretations), create a gap between law or state ordering as it *ought* to be enforced and enacted – law on the books – and law as it is practiced in the daily lives of state agents – law (or state ordering) in motion – law at its capillaries (see Ewick and Silbey, 1998; Smart, 1989). In this slippage lies what we have been calling the discretionary moment: the point in time and place where law is infused with moral content in its most particularized and local form. It is in these discretionary moments that the contextualized field of practical reasoning and local action is revealed, particularly how the fluidity of identities mixes with improvised notions of right and wrong, good and bad, to produce state administration.

This approach to discretion departs from the mainstream in a couple of ways. Mainstream studies, particularly in the field of public administration, focus on the problem of *evaluating* discretionary decisions made by street-level workers. Our approach is to *valuate* these decisions: to examine the interplay of norms, state power and identity. Also mainstream works treat discretion as deviation from law, and a barrier to the 'objective,' or uniform practice of rules. We depart from this notion of law and discretion and instead treat discretion as the interjection of one's self, and the concomitant understandings of others, into the enactment of rules or the making of law.

Musheno (1986) made a break from the mainstream body of inquiry about street-level decision making by arguing that a plurality of decision values – everyday notions about allocating benefits and burdens roughly connected to prevailing notions of justice – drive the everyday decisions of street-level workers. Building on this premise, this book explores how line workers' practices, as culture-in-use and laden with ideological and paradigmatic content about the way things *ought* to be, have the effect of reinforcing those cultural orientations, both for the agent and for other citizens. Moreover, the book traces how normative orientation connects with action, as state actors describe their decisions allocating the state's benefits and burdens to various kinds of citizens (Oberweis and Musheno, 1999). This process is routine, ultimately defining all subjects as *state* subjects, by connecting citizen and state agent in personalized, identified, moralized as well as bureaucratic terms.

Rights Discourses

An important concept in this book is 'right.' In this term, power and morality fuse in the discretion of street-level workers. The historical experience of 'rights' has been different depending on one's social position and visibility before law. Scholars and activists do not share a single understanding of rights and their value for social justice.

People before the Law: Rights and (In)visibility

Although the concept has already taken several turns within the body of sociolegal inquiry, we find it to be quite powerful and, instead of abandoning it, we intend to play on the term in an extended sense throughout the book. Sociolegal treatment of rights has been written in layers. Civil rights have long been widely seen as a key to securing a group identity and therefore gaining full political, democratic membership. Engel and Munger wrote, 'Civil rights are rights of inclusion for the individual whom society otherwise excludes' (1996:10). Without being recognized under the law, entitlement to state benefits could be overlooked. Through legal recognition, individuals become subjects of law: identified political members entitled to the freedom and protection guaranteed by the state. This is a traditional logic, almost common sense. Even by negation, Engel and Munger again summarize the spirit: 'When civil rights are *not* asserted, the consequences can be profound: invisibility, the erasure of the individual from the community's membership list' (ibid.).

But a lack of invisibility is not the same as true equality. This realization has led some to question the ability of rights discourse to accomplish that end and to launch a critique on these grounds. Legal and social power overlap, but do not – indeed, could not – become each other's exact reflection, and there is slippage between law on the books and the actual circumstance of various legal subjects (see Smart, 1989). Historian Jacqueline Jones tells her readers, 'the Civil Rights Act of 1965 failed to reverse historic patterns' that worked to keep blacks 'politically powerless' (1992:276–7). Because the law is enacted and interpreted in social contexts by socially located actors, legal rights alone cannot dismantle systems of racism and sexism.

Critical Legal Studies (called 'CLS') has contributed to the current sociolegal dialogue about rights by extending the critique, explicitly recognizing power as a factor in the experience of rights. Mark Tushnet (1984), among others, argues that rights are unstable and indeterminate. They can (and will) be used to oppress as well as to liberate. He explains that 'the language of rights is so open and indeterminate that opposing parties can use the same language to express their positions. Because rights-talk is indeterminate, it can provide only momentary advantages in ongoing political struggles' (ibid.:1371). Arguments about rights can be coopted and used *against* those who claim disenfranchisement just as easily (and perhaps more successfully) as they can be deployed by the disenfranchised themselves.[3] The clear and undeniable implication is that legislation is not sufficient to effect equality or even equal citizenship. Because of the potential danger in having rights used against a politics of emancipation, some critical legal scholarship suggests that such discourse can and will backfire. In short, some CLS scholars suggest that emancipatory scholarship is best served by abandoning the hope of equality through rights talk.

Still, few modern scholars would argue that disenfranchised groups have gained *nothing* from rights and rights talk. Patricia Williams (1991) insists that rights are important, even if they are unstable and indeterminate. She expands the discussion by adding a notion of identity, suggesting that who one is affects one's perception of rights: 'the battle is not deconstructing rights, in a world of no rights... The argument that rights are disutile, even harmful, trivializes that aspect [rights-lessness] of black experience specifically, as well as that of any person or group whose vulnerability has been truly protected by rights' (ibid.:152). A rejection of rights, in her mind as well as ours, reflects an insensitivity to matters of race and other identity tropes. At the same time, an

exclusive and unqualified embracing of rights disavows the slipperiness of
power exercised in its amorphous, capillary moments.

Rights, Rearticulated

We embrace Williams' thick notion of rights, and draw on an identity-based
framework to strengthen and refine it. Williams argues that one's perspective
of rights depends on who one is, sociopolitically, and we agree. Indeed, this
intermingling of identity with conceptions of rights and their value is precisely
what reinvests the term with a new complexity that opens a place for rights talk
in the broader discourses of legality and the state. By fusing the legalistic term
'rights' with a culturally-driven, identity-based understanding of the meaning
of rights, the already blurry line between law and culture becomes even more
deeply obscured. Conceptualizing rights this way admits culture to law. Along
with a recognition that legislating equality has not been possible thus far, we
embrace a discourse of rights and take it outside an expressly legal arena,
grounded in a framework of cultural identity.

Apart from civil or other legalistic rights, there is a basic epistemological
matter at hand. Getting to questions of how people know what they know,
epistemology forces interrogation of the way people choose between
alternative definitions of what is around them, what is known to be. Competing
claims are not confined to the domain of the judiciary; they shape
interpretations and actions in the everyday, including those of state actors.
Common sense – that set of routine, reflexive judgements – often reveals
which claims to trust and which to ignore. It is this common sense, this
backdrop – this epistemological reflex – to which we apply a notion of rights.
To whom does common sense grant a right to define a situation, an event, a
character? Whose right to know ultimately is taken to be (in effect) true? This
epistemological 'right' to be right helps form the parameters of the decisions
that state actors must routinely make, affecting not only how the state is
administered, but also its freedoms, supports and protections.

We examine work-related stories told by state agents as authoritative
claims about the everyday, or who people are and how events unfold in relation
to the actions of people, including street-level workers themselves. Claims
about the everyday are ranked and hierarchized so that some (people's) claims
count more than others('). These claims are foundational; they both reflect
and create assumptions about what is real, about who people are, and about
what can be expected in any particular situation. We suggest that some
identities come with relatively more cultural rights to know. In short, some
claims about what is real are more powerful by virtue of their source. In
particular, state actors are invested with more authority than other citizens to
define crucial situations: their individualized judgments about whether and

how the power of the state should be applied to any given situation direct whether and how the state's resources are allocated, or whether state coercion is applied. With the identity of state agent comes some degree of right to have one's claims making wield power, a right to be right. Identity, rights and power are entangled.

We draw on non-hypothetical stories that state workers told about interactions with clients, co-workers and superiors. The cultural–legal power of state workers to act upon their own judgments about clients and policies places them in a different authority position than other kinds of citizens. They are able to act upon and enforce their own senses of 'what ought to be done' in specific instances. Claiming the state's authority gives weight to individual agents' claims and enforces this right to be right: the power to define operationally what is.

The Weight of the State Actor's Identity

Scholars of policing have taken note of the weight of state actors' identity. As Tom Ross suggests, 'When the state's agents apply their understanding of law and bring to bear the specter and reality of force and violence that is the state's, this is the *state's law*' (1996:5, original emphasis). Most succinctly, he argues of police that 'the officer's choice becomes the state's law' (ibid.:14). Thus the law is given shape by the uncontrollable humanness of the state agents responsible for making the law concrete in the lives of citizens.

A number of scholars have found that the accounts that state agents offer to explain their actions are infused with moral content. Steve Herbert finds that police officers employ a web of normative orders, or primary values, ranging from law to adventure/machismo (1997:4). He gives significant attention to moral orientation, arguing that 'morality provides a potent self-definition of police' (ibid.:148). Also he intimates that moral orientations, combined with the power of police, provide the normative grist for constituting or re-forming citizens: 'In acting to promote what they define as morally good, police officers attempt to reform the citizenry and, simultaneously, to construct themselves as valuable moral agents' (ibid.:142).

Peter Manning suggests that one prevailing logic about the state is that it is often linked with an 'absolute morality,' one that assumes that 'what is done in the name of and by the agents of the state is by definition the good, the proper, and the aim of the state' (Manning, 1997:21). In other words, many citizens take for granted that what the state does is right and good and done in the name of protecting society's moral codes, even though 'people are aware of an enormous range of definitions' (ibid.:23) of morality. Thus, in his view, a substantial number of citizens assume that the power of the state is the power to serve the truth, the right to know what is right.[4] 'Right' and power are implicitly linked through law and governance.

Manning goes on to suggest that police themselves, as one coercive aspect of the state, function to promote and protect this absolute morality of the state.[5] He writes, 'Policing is an exercise in symbolic demarking of what is immoral, wrong and outside the boundaries of acceptable conduct. It represents the state, morality and standards of civility and decency by which we judge ourselves' (ibid.:319). Although Manning suggests that 'the burden of symbolizing the unity of the moral order cannot be left to a single agency or organ of the government' (ibid.:26), he confines his analysis to the police. We agree that the police are certainly important symbols of moral order, but this task is not the burden of only one state agency. Any agency of control – any state agency which offers and denies services – must also take some part in maintaining a sense of public morality, demonstrated by when, how and why its workers distribute goods and services (ibid.:27). Our project examines two state agencies, one a police department and the other a local office of a state's vocational rehabilitation services administration.[6] Both of these organizations are ultimately locations where law and policy become infused with culture and morals, as reflected in the improvisational acts of state actors as they exercise their right to be right in their day-to-day decision making.

Legalistic normative orders, from the top down, become entangled with moralistic ones, both from the bottom up and from side to side, as workers interact with each other and with their citizenries, and the result is neither law nor order, but a mixture of both, uneven and delivered only in local ways. In this sense, the morality of the state is the morality administered by state agents and, in turn, becomes the state's measure of each citizen's worth in the social order. Understanding this unbalanced process of asserting and sustaining a right to be right is the crux of this research.

Valuating Discretionary Moments

We look at discretionary moments as sites of legal practice, searching for the valuative content of these moments while freeing ourselves from the presuppositions that formal law is or should be the normative guide of these practices. Also we build on another strand of critical sociolegal thought, focusing particularly on the police, that moves away from the idea that there is an externalized body of rules that workers follow in their discretionary moments. Specifically, we are guided by Shearing and Ericson (1991) who critique the scholarship on police decision making that presumes action follows rules, even those scholars who have posited the importance of local rules devised at the organizational level and embedded in a fixed police subculture (see Manning, 1977; Crank, 1998). Rather, they see the police as 'active participants in the construction of action' and view police culture as 'gambits and strategies' rather than some organic whole (Shearing and Ericson, 1991:489).

Our framework, combining identity and moral orientation, embraces a sociology of culture that treats culture as particular, fractured and contingent (see Garfinkel, 1967; Swidler, 1968; Sewell, 1992; Gamson, 1992). It builds on works specific to state workers that depict them as 'both guided and improvisational' (Shearing and Ericson, 1991:500; see also Manning, 1989; Van Maanen, 1978) and which recognize that 'while coherence is at times obvious in the police world ... conflict is always present' (Herbert, 1997:146). It draws on worker stories as a valuable source for gaining access to the 'practical reasoning' of line workers engaged in their trades (see Shearing and Ericson, 1991:482). Other scholars of street-level decision making have observed the centrality of worker stories to the 'craft' of street-level decision making. However, they are reluctant to view this form of communication as constitutive of the practical reasoning of workers, in part because these scholars embrace the importance of rule-driven decision making to liberal democracy (see Bayley and Bittner, 1984).

We do not discount the importance of accountability, particularly police accountability. But we are interested in valuating, not evaluating, street-level decision making. With this focus, and drawing on critical strands of sociolegal thought, we are able to imagine discretion as something other than deviation from law. Specifically, we regard discretionary moments as points of practical reasoning that carry a punch or authoritative claims about the everyday that infuse law with moral content in its most particularlized and local forms. Rather than deviation from law, discretion is a point of constituting law and making the state real for people (see Vinzant and Crothers, 1996:2).

We investigate these discretionary moments, focusing on the inter-connections between identities and moralities and examining how state agents navigate and stage the interconnections of their own identities. How do state actors improvise in such a way that their own notions of the right to be right are incorporated as law in practice, the expression of public policy? How does verbiage about the 'right' thing to do combine with local power in the production of identities of state workers and the citizen subjects over whom workers wield power? What actions flow from the local power of workers to constitute identities and know what is right in situational contexts? How do distinct work sites and occupational differences matter in the way agents reason about and act on fellow workers and citizen subjects? Finally, what does the study of discretionary moments reveal about the plurality of the state and state power?

Overview

In a study of discretionary moments of police officers of the Los Angeles Police Department, Steve Herbert draws attention to the significance of 'the spatial embeddedness of social action' (Herbert, 1997: 20). In his formulation, territorial tactics, or controlling people by controlling territory, are bound up with the deployment of local normative orderings, including particularized notions of morality. We focus instead on the intersection of identity and morality, but we agree that space and place matter. In the next chapter, we provide the spatial contexts of our study, beginning with the urban municipality where the state agents of our study operate and then turning to the two local work sites where the workers of our study congregate, meet, talk and do their paperwork.

The middle chapters of this volume focus on our use of narrative as method and explain the main concepts that guide our interpretations of the stories we collected from state agents. In particular, in Chapter 3, we provide an argument for the use of narrative data as the best choice for inquiry of identity and morality in everyday life. In Chapter 4, we offer our perspective of identity and distinguish it from its treatment in social psychology. Also our notion of identity is brought to bear on the body of literature pertaining to moral decision making. This confrontation leads to a reformulation of moral decision making, one that is sensitive to the Gilligan–Kohlberg dialogues and yet intended as a departure from this important body of work. Notions of moral position, identity and moral decision-making are infused with power; the right to be right emerges as a combined effect of identity, moralizing and power. In Chapters 5 and 6, we analyze the stories first for the identity and moralizing content, and second to compare the practical reasoning of state agents from two occupations, each operating in a distinctive work site.

Notes

1   We use the terms 'state agents,' 'street-level actors,' 'street-level workers,' 'line workers,' and 'line agents' synonymously to refer to the functionaries of state administration who interact directly with citizens in the course of their jobs '...[to] deliver benefits and sanctions which structure and delimit people's lives and opportunities' (Lipsky, 1980:3).
2   By 'moral,' we mean that variable set of mores that are derived from fractured cultures and are used to understand rights and wrongs, as we explain more completely below.
3   For example, although the right to free speech was presumably enacted as a protection of the freedom of expression, it has been successfully deployed to protect intimidation tactics, such as by the Nazi party who marched in Skokie, Illinois (432 U.S. 46, 1988). Similarly, *Hustler* magazine's Larry Flint uses right to free speech rhetoric successfully to protect his magazine (485 U.S. 46), which serves, in particular, the most enfranchised group in the country: white men with material means.

4 Certainly, not all citizens share that idea of police. Again, identity and local knowledge are interdependent. For example, residents of a southern California community both support the police and want police powers curtailed (see Mirande, 1989).
5 His view of police is monolithic. Not all police officers in all situations behave uniformly, as our analysis shows. However, we do find it reasonable to believe that this protection of 'state morality' is the rhetoric of many officers and citizens alike.
6 Relying on the workers' own terminology, we refer to this office throughout the text as Voc Rehab, or VR. The counselors who work there we call Voc Rehab counselors, VR counselors or simply counselors. We refer collectively to all participants as 'line workers,' 'street-level workers' and 'state agents.'

2   The Research Setting: Spaces, Politics and Work Cultures

Cultures of work are particular to workgroups interacting in time and place. Local sites of work are places where shared meanings are derived and where conflicts arise over meaning and purpose. Clearly, street-level workers are guided by leadership styles, professional norms and strategic orientations devised by management. But workers have room to improvise and to negotiate the meaning of work on their own terms as they project who they are and what they stand for, often through interactions with one another, but also in communications with managers, supervisors and citizens. It is this view of organizational culture we took into the field, a view that sees cultures of work as particular, fractured and contingent (see Garfinkel, 1967; Gamson, 1992; Herbert, 1998), as well as both guided and improvisational (Shearing and Ericson, 1991).

With this perspective, we sought out local sites of work where cultures of organization are likely to be seen in rich context. Specifically, regarding the police, we focused on two squads of officers each working a time shift together and operating in defined territories in a single municipality. For VR counselors, we concentrated on a single office in the same municipality whose workers share work space, spend hours together in informal communication, and come together routinely as a group to go over their cases. Both the police and the voc rehab counselors operate in a distinctive part of a municipality in the American Southwest. We begin by depicting the demographics of this municipality with emphasis on the distinctive area that is common to the work groups of both agencies. Also we provide an overview of the political history of the agencies and give attention to the strategic orientations of management specific to our time in the field. We move closer to the places where the work groups operate in the everyday and then bring forward the voices of the workers to reveal their views on the citizens they police, negotiations over the meaning of work, and the relational dynamics of the work groups. As we move from a depiction of the municipality to workplaces, we shift from secondary to primary data sources (see Table 3.1).

The Municipality of Glenville

The general place of inquiry, a municipality which we will call Glenville,[1] lies in the American Southwest, in a growing metropolitan area around Big City. The metropolitan area is roughly covered by Monarch County, whose county seat resides in Big City alongside the state government. Monarch County's 2.1 million people[2] are racially mixed, with a white majority and 16 per cent of the population calling themselves 'of Hispanic Origin,' 3.5 per cent self-identifying as black, and slightly less than 2 per cent defining themselves as American Indian. About 3 per cent of the adults in the county speak little or no English and nearly 10 per cent are bilingual. The high technology industry has brought many professionals into the area and, in 1995, the median household income was $36,049.

Glenville's estimated 158,000 people[3] have much in common with the rest of Monarch County. Aside from the high technology industry, there are also manufacturing, education, commerce and tourism to fuel the economy. Census data show steady population increases since the city's incorporation in 1894. A major university in Glenville brings education dollars to the state, as well as a good deal of funded research integrated with the high technology industry. The city's tourism industry is evidenced by its almost 4700 hotel rooms, with new hotels under construction. Nor are hotels the only thing under construction as the city strives to become a more attractive destination point for tourists. An entire semi-luxury residential area is planned alongside commercial development all along a dry riverbed that is being converted to a town lake.

According to a report by the Institute for Law and Justice, 'At nearly 3800 people per square mile, Glenville is the most densely populated city in the state' (Institute for Law and Justice, 1990:22). And Glenville is continuing to grow. Only 27 per cent of Glenvillers were born in the state, and it remains an attractive place to relocate. Unemployment, at 3.2 per cent in 1995, is slightly lower here than it is in either the Big City metropolitan area (3.8 per cent) or the state as a whole (5.1 per cent). Despite a relatively large number of high-tech jobs, and a reputation for being home to a highly-educated, professional populace, the bulk of Glenville's workers hold service sector jobs (31 per cent of those employed and 37 per cent of the total labor force in 1990).[4] Manufacturing jobs were not far behind, though, accounting for 22 per cent of the employed population and nearly 16 per cent of the total labor force.[5]

The Glenville Municipal Police Department has north and south stations and employs a total of 291 sworn police officers, supervisors and managers[6] to handle its 118,652 citizen-generated calls for service each year.[7] According to department statistics, theft is the most frequently reported crime, but Adam Flood, a senior officer, commented on the increasing urbanness of the area: 'I have seen in the last 17 years, um, every year this place looks more and more like Los Angeles ... crime-wise, population-wise.'

Policing the Two Sides of Glenville

The south side of town is heavily residential and, although nearly half of Glenvillers rent their homes, the south side disproportionately is comprised of owner-occupied, single family houses in subdivisions separated by strip malls. Many of the city's professionals live here: doctors, lawyers and members of the high-technology industries join homeowners' associations and raise children in south Glenville. One officer said in an interview that the south side station, opened in 1995 at a cost of about $4.6 million (*State Republic*, 'Neighborless,' 16 December 1995), was commonly called 'the country club' among north side officers. He said of south side police officers, 'They got it made pretty good down there. Not a whole heck of a lot happens down there. There is some action happening sometimes, but it's pretty quiet the majority of the time.'

Similarly, Officer Sano reported that the south side beats were not necessarily coveted, despite their apparent safety. 'I don't like to work down south and a lot of the guys won't work the southern part of Glenville which is more affluent. The reason I avoid it is because if they complain, you're in trouble.' This officer's experience was such that he believed that complaints from residents of south Glenville were a force to be reckoned with (for example, 'You arrested little Johnny and daddy's a lawyer'). Echoing this sentiment, Officer Sue Wiseberg simply reported, 'As far as the wealthier areas go, they demand more of an officer. They demand attention be given to things that really don't need immediate attention, like barking dogs. They feel like they have more money so you should pay more attention to them.'

Fear of more accountability towards citizens was not the only reason officers preferred the northern beats. The perceived likelihood of boredom was repeated as a motivation for choosing one side of town over the other. Officer Clinton Hinkley explained, 'I prefer being busy. I like the serious crimes. I like investigating the more serious crimes. I like responding to hot calls, you know, with serious crimes in progress. I enjoy doing that.' The north side work culture embraced – even relished – the excitement and machismo of hot pursuit and other dangerous calls. The officers who participated in the study all worked the northern beats and most, if not all, did so by choice. There was a sense of energy among the north side officers, evidenced in a desire to face more 'real' crime, to practice 'real police work' and to be recognized as the face of authority, reducing the likelihood of complaints, especially complaints that would be taken seriously. This was a strong feature of the climate of work in the Patrol North Division.

Site I: The Glenville Police Department, Patrol North Division

The focus of our inquiry, the Patrol North Division, has two patrol sectors, which geographically break down the north end of town into northwest and northeast, and a foot detail to patrol downtown. The north side of Glenville is home to both the university and the popular downtown area, which draws a large weekend crowd. In this section, we take the reader on a tour of Glenville's north side, as it is the territory of the police we study closely.

Patrol North: The West Beat

West of downtown is an industrial area which has become increasingly interspersed with residential neighborhoods, including the planned town lake commercial and residential districts. One patrol officer working a beat on this side of town told us, 'I would have to say the majority of the citizens in [my beat] . . . I'd say 70 per cent of the citizens of [my beat] are at or near the poverty line.' Although this is an overestimate, this area's residents have the lowest median household income of the city, earning significantly less than their south side counterparts and even less than other sections of the north side of town. Vicky Cherwin, another officer working this beat described it as having 'a high, high Hispanic population.' She went on to give a description of the typical criminals in this beat:

> Most of the people we deal with are from broken families, either Hispanic or black. Most of the families we deal with, someone's been involved with drugs, mom or dad or both. There's kids in the family that are going to begin criminal activity very young.[8]

Patrol North: The East Beats

To the east of downtown is the most densely populated area of the city, with apartment complexes surrounding the university and neighborhoods pushing east nearly all the way to the boundary road that divides Glenville from Jefferson City, its easterly neighbor. There are three beats in this east quadrant. A large Hispanic population resides in several neighborhoods both east and west of downtown. One neighborhood, in particular, in the central third of the east quadrant (Beat P), is a very old and well-established Hispanic neighborhood and was the site of Glenville's first real effort at community policing. Sue Wiseberg characterized her citizenry in this beat as 'low income . . . Hispanics and white trash.' She explicitly differentiated between the legal and illegal Hispanics.

OK, well, the wetbacks are illegal aliens and they're hard workers, from what I see, anyway...From what I've come across, they don't do anything wrong...The Hispanics are like the gang people, the local people...So the wetbacks seem like less of a problem to me.

Another officer, who works the southern third of the east quadrant (Beat O, where one of the authors lived, adjoining Beat P), describes his area this way:

We have a lot of transient-type people here. We have a lot of transient hotels. A lot of rental property, so we have a lot of transient population in that respect. We also have a gang out here called 'La Vecindario Loco,'[9] which means 'the crazy neighborhood.' They go by 'LVL.' There's six, seven generations out here so family roots are real deep in this neighborhood as far as those types of people.[10] We have a lot of illegal aliens out here in certain areas in this beat. That's pretty much it. We don't have...We have some middle class people, but not too many. The ones that we do have live in some of your apartment complexes...But most of them are low class and it seems like they're either transients or they've lived here forever.

This is the section of town where Glenville's street prostitution and drug sales are known to be routine, particularly along a stretch of one road lined with motels and trailer parks.

In short, Glenville's north side is urban. North side citizens are reported to be lower-income, transient and, often, non-white, particularly in the way the cops identify the citizenry they police. These demographics seem to draw particular officers to this end of town, contributing to a culture of adventure, machismo and 'real' police work.[11]

Back at the Station

The North Station itself, the only Glenville station until 1995, resides in the downtown area in an impressive building at the foot of the Glenville Butte, an easily recognized city landmark. A large, semi-secure reception desk provides work space for two receptionists and a desk sergeant, whose primary task appears to be handling citizen requests for information. A spacious waiting area and a small public desk with pamphlets, forms and (a lack of) pens fill the rest of the entryway to the station. High ceilings, decorative plants and art hanging on the walls are reminiscent of any other office building, but two doors, both secured with combination locks and buzzers, remind visitors that, despite all appearances, this building is not just any other office building.

Officers and civilian employees alike busily pass through the waiting room, bound either for the security doors which lead to the police divisions and the basement jail or for the unsecured corridor beyond the waiting room, which leads to a few conference rooms and a small vending area. The space is infused with a sense of history by the photos of the current and all prior chiefs and other ranking officers which decorate the walls. A trophy case displays the many awards won over the years by leaders, officers and volunteers with this police force.

A Political History of Glenville's Police Department

Beginning his tenure as chief in the late 1960s, Mark Petersen was wed to a quasi-militaristic authoritarian leadership style. Several officers commented on the extreme disciplinarian style of this chief, right down to militaristic uniforms, which have since been changed. Some had been there to experience it; other, newer officers reinforced the impact that this chief made by recounting stories that predated their employment, but were a strong part of their sense of the history and culture of the department. A younger female sergeant, Wendy Burton, described the former chief this way in an interview:

> traditionally, the autocrats have been in control of the power. [The department has] been dictatorial. It's been ruled by fear. It's been 'stifle and control every aspect of the officer.' If you wanted to take a woman half a block away to a gas station because she's out of gas, you had to ask permission from your supervisor to do that. You had to get permission to do [such] basic things that we treated people like kids under that old regime ...

This leadership style and the chief's emphasis on a system of directed patrol were perceived by some officers to translate to a lower standard of policing. Rob Balinski, a senior officer who began his career in the military, explains:

> OK, the Petersen style of policing was go out, do some directed patrol and answer calls for service. That was it. Blah, blah, blah. Well, directed patrol, which is driving around a neighborhood waiting to catch a burglar, doesn't work because we hardly ever caught burglars that way. And what you do is you end up being stuck inside of a two block area inside of your fifty block area and you're in this two block area, so you're not getting anything done. You're not going out and meeting more of the people that you should be.

Although the officers had very clear parameters about what they should and should not be doing, this was not remembered as a period of excellence either by older or by younger officers.

In 1988, after about 20 years as chief, Petersen retired and was replaced by Russell Saunders, a younger man than Petersen. His style was exactly the opposite of Petersen's and he seems to have been hired in a reaction against

Petersen's autocracy. One of his needs assessment issues was that the department lacked creativity, perhaps as a result of the low discretion of line officers and the 'stifle and control policy' of his predecessor. Sergeant Burton, whose words appear above, also described Chief Saunders' tenure: 'And the next chief came in ... and loosened the reins a lot. So the pendulum swung to the far other side and we have what was called "geographic deployment." That defined the department, but we lost a lot of focus and a lot of direction.'

Under geographic deployment, officers' responsibilities were divided strictly by geography, as the name suggests. This marked an early move towards community-based policing, which would eventually become an important discourse in the halls of this department. Unfortunately, little or no information about the beat and its residents was shared among officers, even among those patrolling the same area. There was a good deal of confusion about to whom officers were accountable and how information about cases, victims and suspects was to be disseminated to other officers. The idea of geographic deployment was not abandoned and has since been integrated into the current management system; however, under Chief Saunders it was riddled with problems. Officer Balinski told us,

> As far as geographic deployment went, I felt that it gave too much freedom to some officers who weren't up to accepting that responsibility or that freedom [of limited accountability] and therefore they slacked off on the work that they should have been doing. Which made more work for other people.

Among the newer officers, too, geographic deployment stands out as an unsuccessful precursor to the current system. Officer Vicky Cherwin told us:

> I was working under that for about six months and at that time, I didn't know enough about it, but there were problems that I could see with it. You know, as basic as not knowing who was supposed to report to who, when kind of thing ... And we struggled as a department just to maintain our job, our task. I mean, our basic task of answering calls for service.

To complicate matters of accountability further, Chief Saunders spent a good deal of time out of town. During a ride along, Sergeant Ledman called Saunder's laissez-faire style 'empowerment by abandonment.'

After only four years as chief, Russell Saunders applied to become police chief in neighboring Jefferson City. He was reportedly departing amicably from the Glenville position in search of new goals. Despite the problems that were depicted by the officers, the Big City newspaper reported that 'Saunders has been praised for his work in developing Glenville's community-based policing program, which also is a high priority in Jefferson City' (*State Republic*, 'Chief,' 10 August 1994). His candidacy for the other chief position was withdrawn when he was appointed to a high-ranking municipal post in Glenville, which he still held during this research.

Saunders' replacement, Jack Mitchell, has tried to strike a balance between Petersen and Saunders. Mitchell had been a Glenville officer himself, for many years. He retired, moved away for a year, and came home to claim a leadership role in the organization which had fostered his career. The *State Republic*, reporting that a new chief had been named, said, 'During its recruitment process, the city stressed a working knowledge of community policing . . . As Glenville's assistant chief from 1988, until he left for Washington, Mitchell helped start a community policing program in the city, something that was not lost on Saunders' (*State Republic*, 'New,' 14 December 1994). With improving the community policing program as a high priority, Mitchell reorganized the patrol division and provided more guidelines for discretionary decisions. Simultaneously, he held street-level workers more accountable and gave them more authority, thus effectively striking the balance he sought between his predecessors' two extremes.

In constructing officer work groups, Mitchell included two dimensions: time of shift and place of patrol. Officers work the same time slot each shift and they also work the same neighborhood on each shift. They report to supervisors in each category, so that there is a beat sergeant, who oversees all the officers patrolling one neighborhood, and a shift or squad supervisor, who is responsible for a group of officers who work a particular time slot. The two supervisors have to agree about the performance evaluation of any employee under them, making officers dually accountable for routine performance. Some of the accountability problems faced by Mitchell's predecessors, although curbed, continue as officers often fail to attend beat meetings, in particular those with neighborhood organizers. The shift ordering seems more organizationally rooted than the place-based ordering.

Another of the changes that Mitchell made has been a clarification of the parameters of acceptable actions, and a simultaneous increase in the degree of officer authority and accountability. Information about people and events is shared across those officers involved in any given neighborhood. Each officer knows what the other officers in the beat have learned. Similarly, officers know who is patrolling the beat next to theirs during their shift. This has been a major improvement over the systems of the two preceding chiefs and has led to good deal of organization and cooperation among officers. This structure has formed a foundation for Glenville's commitment to community policing.

In conjunction with the mild but important restructuring of the patrol division, the new cheif also pushed decision making down to the lowest possible level, increasing officer discretion.

The Current Practice of Policing in Glenville

Community Policing is a philosophy and way of life in Glenville – not a program. It is a proactive, decentralized policing approach designed to reduce crime, disorder, and fear of crime by partnering with the community and undertaking problem solving activities to address public safety issues . . . All of our Officers are Community Policing Officers. (Application for *Excellence in Community Policing* Awards Competition)

The Glenville Police Department is recognized nationally as a progressive leader in the movement towards a new wave of policing: problem-oriented policing practiced in partnership with the communities being served and protected. The department's mission statement asserts that 'the Glenville Police Department in partnership with the citizens of Glenville is committed to improving the quality of life in our city by identifying and resolving public safety concerns' (Glenville Police Department, Community Policing Philosophy Mission Statement). The officers practicing the philosophy claim that they are doing it well. Officer Cherwin told us, 'as I understand it, Glenville is really supposed to be one of the leaders of this thing. I mean we were always getting written up for being one of the most progressive departments where community policing is involved.' The stated goals of Glenville's community policing program include crime fighting, the maintenance of order, the protection of life and property, the prevention of crime and the protection of constitutional guarantees (GPD 'Community Policing Philosophy').

As we mentioned above, the move towards community policing began in 1988, with Chief Saunders and his Assistant Chief Mitchell. In Glenville, community policing is reported to be a philosophy, not a project, as Chief Saunders has repeated. A highly detailed master plan for 'Moving Towards Community Policing' was prepared and added to the host of organizational documents. Within the parameters set in the master plan, all officers were to have attended training to learn the tenets of community policing and to become familiar with the master plan by the summer of 1992.

In 1990, the department received a grant from the Bureau of Justice Assistance to implement a community policing pilot project in one north side beat. Business and residential members of the beat were pre-tested about their attitudes towards police and feelings of safety and other quality of life issues. The tenets of community-based policing were implemented for about one year before the beat members were post-tested. The results were sufficient to warrant a second one-year project in a second beat and to continue the practice in the pilot beat. In 1993, the Glenville Police Department created its citywide Implementation Guide. The pilot beat was used to demonstrate the principles, and all officers were expected to implement them across the whole city.

The community-based policing philosophy is, at least in public discourse, a significant break from traditional policing in that it stresses the importance of officers knowing their communities and residents well. This policing style emphasizes crime prevention more than the reactionary strategy typical of traditional policing. Sergeant Burton said, 'I like it because it gives us the ability to be solution-oriented instead of problem-oriented. It gives us a proactive approach that we're doing something versus a reactive approach where I'm going back over and over and over again.'[12] Officers in Glenville now spend a good deal of their time educating their communities about how to deter criminals: for example, how to landscape in such a way that windows are less accessible or how to disseminate information about crimes around the neighborhood to ensure others' safety.

The 'philosophy' stresses resolving some of the issues that typically lead to crime, particularly repeat crimes. Thus, in theory, the community policing strategy when, say, a barking dog is causing problems involves not only resolving the immediate crisis of quieting the dog, but also structuring a way to repair the damage to the neighbors' relationship with each other. Ideally when the dog barks again, the police will not necessarily become involved, thereby reducing the calls for service. Community policing[13] emphasizes crime prevention more than traditional policing, and this is part of the reason for its rhetoric being so well-praised.

One of the basic goals is to form a partnership between the organized residents of an area (usually home owners and managers of rental properties) and the police so that each side helps the other with its common goal of reducing the number of crime victims. Officer Cherwin, originally trained in the 'philosophy,' told one of us that her job is 'not just going out taking a report, but talking to people . . . community policing is more about dealing with people and forming partnerships, if you will.'

There are several programs which are in place to foster the police–community partnership. Formally, within the police resources, are programs such as the Youth Citizen Police Academy, a program run through the PD's Community Services Department and intended to teach older youths to be 'better informed citizens . . . [who] will be in a position to better understand law enforcement . . . and able to relate their experience to family and friends' (Community Partnership Pamphlet on Youth Citizen Academy). A national neighborhood event was brought to Glenville, during which residents were 'asked to turn on outside lights and spend an evening with neighbors and police . . . National Night Out provides the opportunity for the police and the community to strengthen mutual trust and establish a true partnership' (*State Republic*, 'National,' 2 August 1996).

Two other efforts at building a relationship with (usually stake-holding members of) the community involve communication technology. The police department now has some 30 web pages[14] with current information about the Glenville police, complete with hot links to E-mail addresses which promise return mail (although we received no reply). Finally, in January of 1997, the department undertook a television project: 'an hourlong, live call-in show that is the only one of its kind in the metropolitan area' (*State Republic*, 'TV,' 29 January 1997). Thus the department has made visible strides towards integrating police into its citizens' routine civilian matters, such as social hobbies, the web and television, as well as informing the citizenry about law enforcement. Despite the friendliness of the 'community-policing' presence in the lives of Glenville citizens, it is still a police presence in their lives, one that expands the web of state social control to those citizens who are neither criminal nor victim (yet).

As we mentioned above, Mitchell's officers also enjoyed an increased authority over how their day-to-day work should be done. One senior officer, David Wendell, described it to us.

> Now with community policing, we are – the officers themselves are – using more decision making. They're making more decisions. They're using more discretion. The supervisors are allowing them to do these things, where before, it was a very tight ship. There wasn't much room for discretion. You weren't allowed to make decisions on your own. Well, that has changed a lot. For the most part it's for the better.

With strong encouragement for 'community' partnerships and a working knowledge of their neighborhoods and (at least some of) the residents within them, a final crucial element is granting individual officers the authority to make decisions. The Glenville agency provides street-level workers with precise data about their beats, including crime hotspots and places that generate a high volume of calls. With this information and in alliance with citizen groups (for example, neighborhood block watches) and local businesses, officers are expected to identify recurrent problems and harness the means to resolve them.

But not everyone sees the changes as dramatic. Sergeant Burton commented that problem solving is no novel idea:

> I think good officers have always done community policing. You get to a point where you're tired of going to a certain house over and over again. You're tired of certain calls over and over again. And good officers have always been problem-solving officers. And the only thing we've added to that is made more normal appearance. Instead of doing it on one call, we're gonna do it on a community or on a neighborhood... But it's stuff we've always done... We're just calling it something.

Adam Flood, a senior officer, echoes her remarks:

> I did stuff with the elementary school up in my beat eight years before community policing and Adopt-A-School[15] was ever even thought of, so frankly, with the change in chiefs and different styles and stylishness, community policing is a nice term, but frankly I don't see a big difference. As far as most of us that have been around for a long time, I don't really see a difference... There's differences, but I think the differences are on the administrative side. How they view us, how they let us do our thing.

Thus, despite national recognition for its strides in community policing, the officers practicing this philosophy on a daily basis have mixed feelings about how revolutionary the ideas are.

Nevertheless, one would not wait long after entering the halls of Glenville's police station to hear community policing buzz words. Mission statements, training manuals and other organizational documents are filled with buzz words, too, and the local media have been defining the Glenville PD as a community policing department consistently for several years. Community policing rhetoric, if not some genuine practical changes, is firmly entrenched in the organizational discourse of this department.

Local Culture of Work

Most of the participating officers felt that relations between themselves and their peers were good. One younger, white officer, Marty Forrester told us, 'I think we definitely cooperate with each other and work well together.' Similarly, an older minority officer described worker relations as 'Friendly. We all work together. We're all doing the same thing. We look out for one another. I guess "friendly" would be the best... there's a lot of teamwork involved.' The officers described the whole of the department as being mostly white and male. Many had military experience and several related strongly to their family identities, as parents and spouses. Education level was widely varied, from one story-telling officer holding a Master's degree to others with little or no college experience. This proved to be a topic of heated discussion during our involvement with the department.

There are a large number of sworn female employees in Glenville, considering the historical dominance by males, and, moreover, the women have achieved relatively high rank. At the time this research began, a woman held the highest ranking position in the Patrol Division, as commander. Moreover, she acted as a mentor for women under her, and assisted them in also gaining rank in the division. One participant in this study is a female lieutenant (one rank down from commander) and another is a patrol sergeant (one rank down from lieutenant). Both of these women expressed gratitude to the female commander and were saddened by her retirement, which occurred towards the beginning of our research time.

Glenville does not just support women as non-traditional members of the occupation, but makes clear efforts at supporting lesbian women. These women's sexual identities seem not only to be known among the women, but also suspected by the rest of the department. Other officers seemed not to be significantly bothered by the non-traditional presence. Officer Flood, a long-time member of the force, told us, 'I guess we kind of have a Clinton policy here as far as gays are concerned: don't ask, don't tell. I've never seen it as a problem.' Many of the officers who participated in this project were aware of and accustomed to, their colleagues' identities as lesbians. Of course, some, such as Raymond Carillo, had reservations:

> I'm not sure I would want to be on their bad side... It doesn't bother me as far as work wise... Makes me feel a little leery, me personally... With numbers and positions, you gain power. I don't care what kind of group you are... Within time you will command power. It's hard for me to accept these situations. I wasn't raised that way. It's not my lifestyle. It's hard for me, see, to say I accept it.

This lesbian presence in the department does not negate a simple fact repeated by several officers, in this instance Mani Sano: 'I think that, for the most part, the power in the police department is concentrated amongst the white males.' In fact, it had the unanticipated effect of putting officers of color at odds with white lesbian officers over the issue of hiring. This tension emerged during a first 'ride-along' with one of two black officers on the entire police force and then again within one of this officer's stories, which is detailed in another chapter. To restate, though, most of the officers who participated in the project gave positive evaluations of their peer relationships.

Similarly, most felt quite comfortable with their supervisors. Several officers commented on the open door policy of the chief and recognized an informal invitation to speak directly to members of the command staff. Adam Flood commented, 'I feel like I could walk into the chief's office. I mean I remember the chief when he was Jack, and he still is. And all the commanders.' While not everyone expressed this comfort level, many officers indicated that they could voice opinions and complaints to their superiors, even several levels up the chain of command. Officer Wendell told us of lower level managers, 'practically all of the patrol supervisors are pretty good. They work with you. They try to help you improve as an officer.'

Men who worked under the female sergeant who participated in the study also denied any problems working for her. Officer Balinski responded this way about the general feeling:

> Anything difficult? No, actually I don't. Maybe in another police organization that might be, maybe in a larger organization, but in our department, we have ... when someone gets promoted to sergeant ... I just think we're more professional. When someone gets promoted to sergeant if they treat you decently, then they're going to get the respect of the line officers.[16]

In short, gender relations were strong in the department, and it did not appear that the significant presence of women, lesbian women in particular, caused any major disruption either among the workers' peer relationships or between workers and their supervisors.[17] However, Officer Cherwin did tell a story that was very explicitly about sexist selections for special assignment teams. This story, which is detailed in a later chapter, was corroborated by other, male officers as well. She stressed that she felt her organization was not sexist as a whole, despite its problematic selection process for special assignments.

Unlike the sex or sexual preference of employees, race seemed to be a charged topic.[18] Glenville has a low number of minority officers, male and female. The city's large Hispanic population (almost 15 per cent of the city's total population[19]) and its small number of Mexican and Spanish-speaking officers created communication problems. The language barrier was presumed to alienate some Glenvillers from the police and lower the reporting of crimes victimizing non-English-speaking residents.[20] The participants seemed to agree on this much, although Officer Clinton Hinkley tried to justify the lack of black and Hispanic officers with arguments which are, by now, familiar:[21]

> We don't really have a whole lot of mixes. The majority of them are white males ... I guess those other races of people who test just don't do well. I guess looking at it from the outside, it looks pretty bad. You know, we only have three black male officers?[22] Are we a racial department or ... You know, there's got to be a reason. Well, yeah, the reason is because the people we have testing for our department just don't do well.

One African–American officer addressed the topic directly and had several comments to make. Early in our relationship with this officer, he told us that the racial balance in the department was 'off-kilter.' He explained that there had been a total of three black officers during his time at the department and that he had taken the issue of hiring minorities as a pet project. He expressed strong frustration in his department's unwillingness to hire black officers, and clearly did not believe that it was lack of qualified people. Instead, he attributed it to the department's recruitment system, among other factors.

Meanwhile, this officer also described complications within the department as the result of racism: 'I have experienced racism both outside the department and inside.' He got little satisfaction when he complained to his superior years ago that a colleague had called him 'nigger.' The sergeant first tried to ignore the situation, but then he separated the two officers and reprimanded no one. A second officer, Ray Carillo, had a problem with a racist colleague, but again the supervisor dismissed it. 'I did a long time ago and when I complained to the supervisor about it, he ignored it.' Moreover, the black officer related an added stress to his job:

> I've always had to be under self-control a lot more than other officers because of my being a minority. If I fly off the handle and lose control, then I'm labeled as the black officer who can't handle it. That's always been a pressure on me, but I've been able to handle it so far.

Officers also believed that other local police and emergency work agencies, and perhaps even the people of Glenville, might think the department was racist. The department clearly has a reputation for being racist. One officer said, 'There's a feeling in the department that they don't like Mexicans, they don't like blacks.' Two other officers made similar comments.

In addition to the participants reporting this perception, there is outside evidence that a certain amount of racism was part of the organizational culture. In March of 1996, the *Glenville Tribune* reported that several Hispanics, each of whom thought he or she 'would be treated as a US citizen with rights,' gathered together in public protest to relay 'their stories of alleged police harassment.' They said police 'illegally questioned their resident status' (*Glenville Tribune*, 'Actions,' 15 March 1996). In addition, the city lost a civil suit in June of the same year. Although the department was not held accountable for charges of anti-Semitism, it was found to have 'violated the civil rights of two former bar owners' who were Jewish and asserted their case in the words of anti-Semitism (*Glenville Tribune*, 'Bar,' 7 June 1996).

Despite the newspaper's promise the following week that, 'The Glenville Police Department will review its basic procedures following a federal judge's ruling' (*Glenville Tribune*, 'Ready,' 16 June 1996), still the informal culture was decidedly tolerant of some racism. In October of 1996, while this research was under way, in a *Tribune* article criticizing the department's numbers of women and minorities on the Glenville force, Chief Jack Mitchell is quoted as saying, 'Obviously we need to have equal representation, and obviously that's what we need to work on' (*Glenville Tribune*, 'Short,' 12 October 1996). The problem, recognized by some officers as well as the media, was also recognized by the chief, but no immediate solutions were at hand.

Contrary to the seemingly strong sentiment that relations between workers and supervisors were good, there was a newly born but quite popular workers' union among officers. In November of 1996, the *Tribune* reported, 'So far, the Glenville Officer Association has 130 members, a majority of the department's sworn officers' (*Glenville Tribune*, 'Union,' 7 November 1996).

Our period of observation saw the union unfold and become affiliated with other unions, one a fire-fighting union in neighboring Jefferson City and the other a police union for the much larger Big City Department. The acting president, founder and spirited leader was one of the participants in this project. Some of the officers' concerns include street-level officer pay, legal representation for officers and increasing street-level power in making department decisions, such as whether there should be educational requirements for officers.

Summary of Glenville PD

Generally, street police officers tend to focus on relational dynamics among themselves in articulating the culture of work. While they are aware of the priority management gives to community policing, they remain focused on valuating one another, and on 'talking up' their desire to police the north side because of opportunities for adventure, or 'real' law enforcement work. Peer relations among officers were usually described positively, with a high degree of confidence that, should an emergency arise, strong support would be on-site immediately, regardless of the requesting officer's gender, race or sexual orientation. Similarly, participating officers largely described their relationships with supervisors as a two-way trust system. Many officers confidently broke away from the traditional senior–subordinate relationship and routinely asked for advice about cases, knowing that there would be no repercussions, only guidance. Conversely, sergeants in particular seemed to back their subordinates' decisions both to the public and to the command staff. Routine decision making was effectively distributed to the lower rungs of the hierarchy, although it was tempered with daily briefings about the department's priorities in law enforcement and expenditure of time and resources.

Still, some tensions surrounding identity and personal difference clearly emerged. Although many officers expressed little concern about working with the relatively large number of women and gays, there was some uneasiness about this. Race, as well, created some tensions in the department, in terms of both peer relations and relations with superiors, when complaints of racism were not taken seriously by managers. Generally, this was remedied by silence. Sergeant Burton, who is a lesbian, said, 'We have not integrated social groups in the department to where, you know, people are comfortable asking other people about their culture, being a part of their culture ... I think we're very segregated and that also has an effect on the community we serve.' The most apparent evidence of this effect is a language barrier foreclosing the possibility of any communication with a whole segment of the population. Internally, too, the birth of the union must be taken as evidence of conflict in the department.

Finally, there is a tacit conflict between the air of adventure and machismo that explicitly guided the officers' preference to work the north side of the city and management's high-priority commitment to community-based policing. Officers were proud of their willingness – in fact preference – to fight dangerous criminals and, at the same time, paid at least verbal homage to the philosophy that made their department nationally noteworthy. This contradiction was unstated, and perhaps unnoticed, by the officers of Glenville.

State Rehabilitation Services Administration

Unlike the GPD, the state Rehabilitation Services Administration (RSA) serves a particular population. Of the more than 1.3 million people in Monarch County between the typical work ages of 16 and 64, about 7 per cent live with disabilities.[23] About 3 per cent are prevented from working, leaving a total of 4 per cent of the population who are living with disabilities, but able to work. These are primarily the clients of the local branch of the RSA. The state organization's mission statement reads, 'The mission of the Rehabilitation Services Administration (RSA) is to work with individuals with disabilities to achieve increased independence and/or gainful employment through the provision of comprehensive rehabilitative and employment support services in a partnership with all stakeholders' (*Handbook for Applicants*, 1).

As a branch of the state's Department of Economic Services (DES), RSA is a statewide organization, linked with other similar organizations in other states by federal laws and funds, as well as transferring clients.[24] It offers three basic services to those with disabilities: Vocational Rehabilitation (VR), Independent Living Rehabilitation Services (ILRS) and Economic Support Services (ESS). The Glenville office which participated in the project was a specialized office. Only one Economic Support counselor worked within the office, and the most senior staff member was the only Independent Living counselor at the office. Apart from the clerical staff, the rest of the office was dedicated to VR.

The Vocational Rehabilitation Program, by definition, 'helps people with disabilities become or remain economically independent through work' (VR Program Description). To be eligible, a person must first have documentation of the disability and, second, must be better able to get or keep a job as a result of services. These extremely broad eligibility requirements essentially allow anyone with a documented disability to be made eligible for services. However, the research team found that people were screened when they initially called in. Some were offered appointments with counselors and others were told that VR could not or would not help them.

Typical VR services include equipment for accommodating disabilities (such as hearing aids or, often, clothes for those with mental illnesses) and job assistance in the form of updated job training, vocational counseling, job placement and job counseling to help keep the client at work, once placed. Clients often come in hoping for full college tuition coverage, which is not outside the domain of potential benefits, but was rarely given during our period of observation.

Site II: The Glenville RSA Office

We focused on the Glenville office of RSA, which was housed in a relatively large, modern concrete building and lies on the road which the police use to divide Glenville into north and south. As one approaches the building from the parking lot, its U shape becomes apparent and one enters the courtyard that fills the inside of the U. There are cement benches and staircases here, where the working smokers can be found taking breaks and chatting with one another. Several of our observation periods ended here, in the courtyard, sharing a cigarette break with the supervisor of the RSA office. The glass door to the office, equipped for wheelchair access, is undramatic, like the rest of the office, and leads to a set of offices off a circular hallway. The center of the circle houses a rest room (large enough to admit a wheelchair), which doubles as a storage closet (diminishing the likelihood of passage by wheelchair), and a small, but complete, kitchen. Individual offices, all with florescent lighting, fill the perimeter of the circle and, though the carpet is old, the paint is fresh and the place smells not musty, but papery.

The foyer, which is also the waiting room, is dominated by a reception desk, which was not staffed even once during the seven months we visited there. Katrin, the administrative secretary, sits in a large office with a sliding window looking into the foyer. There are two office waiting-room chairs between two tables displaying a myriad public service pamphlets. A second office has windows looking out into the waiting area, this one belonging to the office's sole Independent Living counselor. The circular corridor is wide, presumably to permit passage by wheelchair. One of the offices has been transformed into a conference room, simply by filling it with a conference table too big for the room, but barely big enough to seat all the staff members. Employee mailboxes are in this conference room, which is convenient owing to an almost endless supply of handouts that are distributed during the weekly staff meetings alone.

The walls are covered with an interesting and quite personalized array of decorations. One gay counselor had several pieces around her office with rainbows and pro-diversity messages. Another counselor placed 'junk-art' trinkets all around her office, some of which she had made herself. The administrative secretary had a passion for Marilyn Monroe, whose face peered out from all around his office, in frames, on magnets, on his calendar, and, most prominently, from a life-sized cut-out which stood, forward-leaning and underdressed, in his window. Even the corridor was decorated with a poster supporting women's professional basketball. The staff, as a whole, seemed quite comfortable with the array of styles and attitudes of its members, and not in terms of decoration alone. We will return to this tolerance below, after explaining some of the historical politics which shaped office relations.

Prior to our involvement with the Glenville office, there had been some changes in leadership. Less than a year before we met the participants, they had been working under a much liked office supervisor, Frank King. Over the last year, management had changed twice, the office had been redefined in terms of its client base, and several new counselors had joined the staff, either from other offices or as totally new counselors. Only about half of the staff remembered working through two changes in leadership, but nearly everyone who participated in the project was aware of that shift.

King was remembered lovingly by staff veterans. Repeatedly, participants described his office style as 'family-like.' A rehab technician,[25] who we will call Carey, remembered him fondly:

> He went to my wedding . . . he was always, you know, keeping in touch to see how I was feeling. You know, I really had a lot of contact with him. And, um, like office parties, most of the time were, like, held at his house. He held us very close in like a family way.

Despite his employees' strong positive feelings, Carey went on to say that King was put (apparently involuntarily) on administrative leave and that 'he quit, I think, but eventually he was going to be fired . . . some policy issue that he did not follow.' Another counselor was equally vague about why the much-loved supervisor left the office: 'Two weeks after I started, the supervisor retired or left or I don't really know.'

Frank King left before a formal replacement could be found, and so the senior counselor at the office, who specialized in Independent Living, became the acting supervisor. She was passive in the role and, as a result, the office lost its direction. After the consistency of the much-loved supervisor and the passivity of the interim one, the new supervisor, Jane, was, by all accounts, treated with caution and a certain amount of mistrust. However, Jane's long history with RSA, her great knowledge of the details of a whole host of disabilities, and her strong but gentle leadership style quickly won her most of the employees' confidence. Rather than a family leader, her employees see her as a professional leader. One VR counselor, Benita, sums up the whole transition this way:

I know that this office went through, like I said, this outted supervisor and we became even more independent when we didn't have that. So that was a little rough. That Jane is very much by-the-book. She's very professional and she knows what she's doing.

As Jane came in, the office was organizationally redefined to be a specialized RSA center, emphasizing care for persons with severe mental illnesses. Thus three VR counselors of the five there, plus half the time of the rehab tech, are dedicated to serving the severely mentally ill. Because the office was redesignated, several new counselors started working at that office, coinciding with Jane's arrival. This had the effect of ensuring that at least some of the staff identified only Jane as the office leader. These newer counselors, overwhelmed by the enormous amount of information to be absorbed and put into immediate use, explicitly appreciated Jane's wide knowledge of both the disabilities and RSA policies and practices. One counselor, named Betty, who actually transferred from another office with Jane, said, 'She's very understanding. Because I come in and, you know, ask her tons of questions because there's so much to learn.'

Presumably in an effort to mildly homogenize office practices, Jane has weekly staff meetings, in which counselors share their cases with each other. Not only does this give her more control over how her office runs, but it serves as a teaching process for the newer counselors and simultaneously opens communication about cases between counselors. Although most of the counselors had some previous work experience that was related (such as working for an assisted living home for people living with disability or working for a private institution to ease the transition to independent living), RSA itself inundated its counselors with endless pages of new codes, policies and procedures. These were often reviewed in staff meetings.

The atmosphere of the meetings was always friendly, and staff members were nearly always on time and often arrived in the conference room early. During the staff meetings, birthdays were celebrated, vacation souvenirs shared, and co-workers invited each other to parties. From the staff meetings alone, little dissension among the counselors could be detected. A division between the veterans and the novices was evidenced only in who gave rather than received advice, although the newer counselors did not seem shy about brainstorming on a veteran counselor's case.

In addition to this ability to work together gracefully, the staff also seemed to share recreation. During our first few visits, there was talk of going to the movies and of having a Fourth of July party.[26] Lunch was an important part of peer relations, "cause most of us just stop at twelve and eat lunch together,' Carey, the rehab tech, said. Benita, who was a newer counselor, also described her peer relations in terms of lunch.

> I mean, you'll have your little lunch crowd that...people just have more in common. And we make fun of it, actually because Betty and Sharon are both vegetarians. And, you know, I'm no vegetarian, so we're having like the red meat – but I think it's a respectful atmosphere which makes it nice.

Her words reveal an office that is aware of its differences: vegetarians and meat eaters, male and female, lesbian and straight, black, Hispanic and white, able-bodied and disabled, senior and newer counselors, counselors for the severely mentally ill and the other kinds of counselors. Several counselors revealed their awareness of the differences among them, but commented on the professional or respectful way they were handled. The only male counselor (of seven counselors plus one supervisor), Thomas, describes the same idea: 'Even in spite of maybe we have some differences, I think we try to work on those and act professionally.'

However, this same counselor was apparently somewhat oblivious to some differences, as he went on to say, 'We have had ... in terms of individuals who have disabilities, who have worked here, we don't have anybody, but we have had in the past... That was really helpful, having her inside and her situation. Consult with her on cases...' However, his comment overlooks the fact that two of his colleagues are living with disabilities, one hard of hearing, the other able to use only one of her eyes.[27]

The office was divided in terms of old staff (those who remembered the family-oriented supervisor) and the new staff (those who came around the same time as the new supervisor and mostly focused on the severely mentally ill). Contributing to the division was the fact that at least two of the newer counselors, who both work with the severely mentally ill (hereafter SMI), spend half their time in a completely different agency. Although each has an office space at the Glenville VR office, they also share another office in a Mental Health Services building, working with case managers on cases that require cooperative efforts with ComServe, the state-contracted, privately run mental health facility. The result is that, as Betty said, 'A lot of times we don't see each other that much because we're all gone at different times in the day. When we're here, we're usually working on the computer.'

Similar to Sharon and Betty, the Independent Living counselor, Kathy, was also out of the office a great deal, inspecting homes and vehicles and attending new clients still hospitalized after the disabling event. Only a few of the staff members were actually in the office 40 hours a week, and perhaps this contributed to a sense of alienation compared to life under the previous supervisor, when the office was not specialized for severe mental illness cases and the staff worked more uniform hours in the office together.

There were other social differences at work, too. Two female counselors are openly gay. Only two men work in the office. One is a counselor and the other is an administrative secretarial manager. One man is black; two women are Hispanic and one woman is Jewish. The other six are white. Two women live with disabilities and a third lives with a disabled partner. For such a small group of people, there were many social differences, and it seems that many of these differences are quite new to the office.

Thomas expressed some dissatisfaction with the way the new supervisor had conducted the recent hiring:

> I know that the previous supervisor had, you know, a philosophy about hiring people and he was a very family-oriented man and I think he looked at that and he looked at the situation and the personalities meshing together . . . and I don't know that that is still a consideration. Um, there's a different dynamic going on now.

He implied later that the different dynamic was about hiring different kinds of people in an affirmative action sense, and he was open to the possibility that this was mandated from above, rather than Jane's own agenda. His reference to the 'family-orientation' of the previous supervisor is ambiguous, possibly referring to personalities, but also possibly referring to identity conflicts, as a mild rejection of the lesbian counselors who comprised about half the new hires. One of these gay counselors voiced a mild complaint about Thomas, too, saying that his general caseload made him seem like a better counselor because he was not plagued by the relapses typical of her severely mentally ill clients.

It seems to us that the small number of people working in the office contributed to an atmosphere which resembled that between siblings: counselors basically protected each other from outsiders, like us, and praised each other as professional and respectful, but day-to-day relations were probably sometimes charged with an air of spirited disagreement or mild competition. This family-like system is ironic, given how distressed veteran office members were at the loss of such a family orientation when King left. Rather than his nuclear family, the office 'family' now operated under Jane's professional leadership, sibling peer relations and a new diversity. This new family orientation was most difficult for Thomas, the sole male counselor, with a general caseload and a good deal of seniority.[28]

Despite any groupings and problems among the staff members, discourse was open and honest. One of the two lesbian counselors told us, 'Everybody is supportive of Nicole and I[29] and our relationship. They incorporate us, as a couple, in terms of office gatherings and that is very, very cool because you never know how an office as a whole is gonna react.' Thus, for all the awareness of the identity differences among them, the staff as a whole is judged to be supportive and inclusive. The culture of the office seemed to be one that was both sensitive to difference and yet ultimately willing to get past it and recognize that, 'Hey, we're all here for the same reason.' The hard of hearing counselor, Judy, commented that

> it's been sufferable sometimes but this is also a very supportive, warm environment... Um, I find these people, in this office particularly, willing to work with me, knowing that if they start talking to me after I leave the room I won't respond. It's nice to have that consideration for a change, on the job... they don't complain about me not answering the phone all the time because I didn't hear it or something but rather work with me to meet my needs.

Counselors for the severely mentally ill had to reconsider definitions of 'success' in any given case. Organizationally, in a whole series of numeric codes assigned to various case statuses, a '26' meant that the case was closed successfully: the person had been placed in a job and seemed able to maintain that job without extended support from RSA. A counselor's promotability was determined primarily on the number of clients each year who reached status 26. In the case of the severely mentally ill, a dilemma arises for counselors. Because the illnesses tended to be cyclical, a client could do well for a while, only to have things fall apart as the disease makes itself active again. Jane tells a story which exemplifies this very common problem.

> *Leigh was then placed in another temp-to-hire position at a local heart clinic. After working there about 8 months, she was offered a position... Upon Leigh talking to her supervisor, they did eventually hire her... Leigh's illness was such that most of the time, she did not recognize she was beginning to cycle. Typically, she would become paranoid at work, thinking people were talking about her. Then relationships [would start] falling apart and she would end up either getting fired or quitting.*[30]

It was tempting for counselors to put cases into 26 status when the illness was stabilized, remove the extended supports and allow the disease to cycle again, and eventually reopen the case, restarting the whole cycle.[31]

In addition, counselors pointed to a desire to advocate for clients and go beyond the job parameters. Benita said,

> I think that counselors... really have to struggle with that balance because we have a tendency to want to go above and beyond because we all kind of have this advocacy in us. You know... they cannot advocate for themselves, so you just naturally want to do that... And then we're state employees. You know, there are very defined roles in what we're supposed to do. You know, our job is to try to get these people employed and to try to maintain employment. So I think that there's a constant struggle, you know.

Similarly, Judy extended her job parameters to include assisting the hearing-impaired and deaf clients with cultural issues that go well beyond employment in a strict sense and push the boundaries of her job.

> I'm also dealing with cultural issues. Deaf culture has its own identity that's completely different from hearing culture... they'll [have to] be able to work in the hearing culture because they're the ones that have the money, not the deaf culture... It's a long, drawn out, complex process.

Thus finding jobs for clients was often seen as a second layer in the rehabilitative process, and there were often several layers after job placement as well. These extended services usually amounted to weekly attention, just to make sure no problems were arising between clients and employers. This was usually critical, and was often the point of relapse for many SMI clients.

Because such a small number of clients, especially mentally ill clients, were able to be placed successfully in jobs and to keep those jobs independently, success had to be redefined in the counselors' own way. Benita told me that success, for her, was a sense of empowering clients: 'it's just the feeling you get when you employ somebody and then just to see them become so empowered and say, you know, "God, I have options in this life" and, you know, it's pretty incredible.' To her, success could even fly in the face of the RSA mission:

> And then not everybody's ready to work. And when they realize that, that it's OK not to work, that this is not going to make them or break them, that's a success. I mean, you might not get them a job, but they know that it's OK, and that they're doing fine, and... that they're just productive people.

Improving clients' self-esteem was often identified as a success criterion. Moreover, this office interpreted the rules in such a way that VR money was spent to achieve a self-esteem goal, whether or not this was absolutely necessary for work-related goals. Benita told a story about one such client.

> *When I mentioned dental exam, her eyes lit up and she smiled (immediately covering her mouth with her hand)... I went on to explain that sometimes when people have missing teeth, it affects their confidence level and they tend to be socially withdrawn... To get $1500 of dental treatment authorized from the agency can sometimes be risky. Comments I've heard in the past are, 'She doesn't need teeth to work,' 'How do we know she won't quit?,' 'She won't appreciate it.' Although my beliefs conflicted with the agency's informal policies, I felt Carol deserved a chance at self-esteem and success with employment. I feel $1500 is a small price to pay for a life altering change.*

In this same spirit of deprioritizing RSA's mission within the office, we observed a highly flexible set of criteria for eligibility. Recall that the criteria were simply that the person have a documented disability and that he or she could benefit from services. Being able to benefit from services was interpreted as 'benefited in the short term,' to be more inclusive. For example, someone who could not be permanently helped could benefit in the short term from things like new clothes or eyeglasses or vocational counseling. This created a situation in which clients who were very unlikely to achieve level 26 status were consistently made eligible for services and granted whatever RSA resources were available. This happened despite the impact such unlikely cases had on the official 'success' rates either of the individual counselors involved or of the office as a whole.[32]

This inclusiveness also indicates one final interesting element of the culture of work in the Glenville office. Unlike what we expected from a government-run, social services institution, there was basically no shortage of funds. Admittedly, counselors had full caseloads, with some more full than others, but there was generally no problem supplying the resources to fit the cases. Certainly, very few clients had their college tuition paid for by the state through RSA funds, but nearly everyone was given an opportunity to get what he or she needed to get at least an entry level position and sometimes much more than that.[33] Even though the needs of deaf and hearing-impaired clients were proportionally more costly than other kinds of clients, they often got what they needed, as the budgets were evaluated throughout the fiscal quarter and any extra funds in one counselor's budget could often be put towards the budget for the deaf and hearing-impaired.

In sum, at RSA, new policies and regulations were constant, and so were ways to customize those policies. Jane ran the office as predictably as possible, and this was recognized by the counselors, nearly all of whom eventually came to trust her and to respect her vast knowledge of the field. There was some remaining mistrust, in particular from the one male counselor. He preferred discussing his cases with another senior counselor (who was also female) rather than approaching the supervisor for advice, but even he acknowledged her credibility and experience. The few people working in the office generated some interpersonal tensions, but all accounts indicate that staff members related to each other well and welcomed each other's questions and opinions about cases.

Later, in Chapter 6, we delve deeper into the cultures of work of the squads of officers working Glenville's north side station house and VR counselors of the Glenville branch of RSA. Our deeper exploration of the cultures of work draws on stories and addresses the intersections of identity, power and moral orientation. Therefore we turn first to our use of experiential data and treatment of identity and morality.

Notes

1 All names are pseudonyms.
2 The following Monarch County statistics are from the 1990 US Census Data (Database C90STF3A), except where noted.
3 1995 City of Glenville Statistical Report and the 1990 Decennial Census.
4 1990 Decennial Census, as reported in the 1995 City of Glenville Statistics.
5 Ibid. The labor force numbers include all workers, regardless of employment status, while the other figure includes only those currently employed.
6 'Glenville in Touch,' Overview of Glenville Police Department, City home page.
7 Ibid.
8 We point out that there is selection bias in who the officer 'deals with' and that this is not necessarily the typical north side resident.
9 The officer actually called the gang 'La Victoria Locos,' misunderstanding the Spanish words.
10 We can only assume he meant Hispanics, collectively.
11 Steve Herbert (1997:79–98) found that street cops working for the Los Angeles Police Department value adventure and machismo. In his account, these norms conflict with 'law' and 'bureaucratic control,' norms preferred by managers of the department.
12 The irony here is that community policing is also often called 'problem-oriented policing.' We are assuming she was praising the philosophy for its attention to problem *resolutions*, rather than merely problems.
13 Some scholars treat community policing as institutional rhetoric intended to restore legitimacy to municipal police agencies that lost standing owing to the failed promises of professional policing. See, for example, Crank (1994). Others focus on the workings of community policing, particularly how police constitute and control 'communities' of involved citizens (see Lyons, 1999) and implementation strategies (for example, Skogan and Hartnett, 1997).
14 According to the *State Republic*, 'Online,' 16 March 1996.
15 Adopt-A-School is another project affiliated with the community policing philosophy, designed to create interactions and trust building between police and local youths.
16 We cannot help but add that even as this officer told one of us – the female one – how his female supervisor was treated normally, he caught himself using a male-oriented term which he felt was rude for female company, and he promptly apologized: 'If they're a dick . . . I'm sorry about that one . . . .'
17 Our timing may have been responsible for this. At the time the research began, the highest ranking officer in the entire patrol division was a lesbian. She was well respected by her subordinates and was very conscientious with other lesbians in the department. She seems to have mentored other lesbians of rank in the department. Our speculation is that the number, placement and seniority of these women had the effect of normalizing the department as a whole to the lesbian presence.
18 One officer, in particular, illustrates this. He was very involved in trying to recruit and hire more minority officers; it seemed to be his pet issue. If anyone had had an axe to grind in competition with the lesbians, it might have been him. Yet fieldnotes from ride-alongs with him read, 'Despite the juxtaposition of lesbians against minorities in the workforce, David was clearly not opposed to the lesbians. He only wanted to add more people of color.' Perhaps because the group of lesbians were well established throughout the ranks it had become normalized. This is our speculation about the unlikely acceptance of these women in an otherwise little-diversified organization.
19 1997 City of Glenville Statistical Report.

20 The fact that some of these Hispanics were illegal was also presumed to lower the likelihood of reporting their victimization.

21 We must insist that this argument is simply not credible to us.

22 Actually, the participating black officer told us there were only two black male officers, and no African–American female officers at that time. During his decade and a half tenure at Glenville, there had been a total of three black officers, including the two currently employed there, and no black female officers.

23 1990 US Census Data, database C90STF3A, for Monarch County.

24 More than one counselor mentioned clients moving around the state or country. Often the old and new VR counselor shared information about the client as they transferred, but it was said repeatedly that other counselors' information was not immediately trusted.

25 A rehab tech is between a rehab counselor and a secretary. This one had recently been promoted from secretary. Her new job gave her increased direct contact with and more responsibility for clients.

26 One of us was sometimes invited to come along as well. We did not visit the office together, and so different relationships developed. Several of the counselors were close to Trish's age and were very friendly towards her, including her in light conversations, inviting her to join in their activities, sharing politics and insights with her, sometimes via E-mail. One counselor still E-mails Trish now, over two years later, about women's rights matters, her side business of selling artistic items, and even personal changes. The relationships with these participants developed very quickly compared to those of the PD, and Trish felt the relationships to be stronger and more open with the VR participants. We suspect the size of each organization played a role in this, among other things. The tone of the two sections should reflect for the reader the tone of our experiences with each organization.

27 Thus, despite the frequent reference to how professional peer relations were, we have some doubt as to the extent of those relations.

28 In fact, between the period of observation and the writing of this volume, he left the office and went to another one.

29 Nicole did not work at the office. She was invited to all social events, like any other spouse.

30 Italics indicate passages taken verbatim from the transformed versions of the workers' stories. (See Chapter 3, note 9.)

31 Fieldnotes from sessions with Benita reflect this conundrum for counselors: 'Because SMI clients tend to cycle, 90 days at a job without successful rehabilitation is entirely possible. Witholding extended support . . . sets a client up for failure – after they've been counted as a success. Then the client returns to RSA and starts all over again. So a counselor could get the points for a 26 more than once for the same client, as the case is opened, closed and then re-opened.' Benita said immediately that it was a conflict of interest.

32 This also has interesting repercussions for taxpayers. Public funds designated to help reintegrate persons living with disabilities into the workplace were being spent on clients with little or no chance of becoming reintegrated.

33 Clients were surprisingly diverse. One client was even described as holding a Ph.D. Thus their placement levels often had to do with what skills they brought to RSA rather than what skills they learned through RSA.

3 Studying Experience and Identity

Studying personal experience offers a window into the meaning and importance of identity in individuals' lives. However, the notion of 'experience' is already riddled with cultural cues and understandings which must be explored and evaluated before experience can rightly be trusted as a foundation for knowledge. Our research relies heavily on experience as data, in the forms of interviews with state workers, stories told to us by the workers, and our own experience of the research as captured in our fieldnotes and subsequent discussions about 'what happened' during our period of inquiry. Given our heavy emphasis on learning through others' experiences as well as our own claims to know based on our participant–observer experiences, it therefore seems particularly important to investigate thoroughly the criticisms of experiential data and to address them clearly.

Experience is Socially Constructed

Experiencing culture is fundamentally creative. What we recognize, record and remember as our 'experience' does not refer to the totality of events that happen in an objective reality; 'experiences' are always already burdened with a social framework by the time social actors are able to identify certain events as their 'experiences.' From the fleeting mass of events occurring around us – from subatomic motion, to planetary trajectories and all the earthly actions between – some events and aspects are selected for perception and others are not. The first filter from 'reality' is the limits of human perceptions: that which we cannot or do not perceive can hardly be counted as experience.

From those events or aspects that are perceived, many are immediately forgotten or disregarded, for we do not have the words to give them definition and lasting existence as 'experience.' What human actors are able to recognize as experience is thus filtered again, this time through language. This is

39

particularly important: what might otherwise be a disorganized set of events and sensory perceptions is fettered to the limited and therefore limiting framework of language. We disregard much of what we cannot name. Furthermore, not only do we disregard what we cannot translate into language, we must also generally be able to translate into *our own* language, one that is bound to our collective knowledge base, needs and broad social framework. Thus communication acts to shape and define our experience even before it acts as the conduit for sharing those experiences with others.

In this poststructural sense, experience is framed and filtered, always already tied to and tainted by social and cultural orders: neither individual nor a connection to objective reality. Thus research methods that involve the study of experience must reconcile that gap between what is being analyzed (the experience) and what is being revealed in the analysis (something about individual experience, but also something about the cultural and social context of that experience). Experience may continue to be highly useful in social science research, although perhaps not in the way we traditionally imagine it. Indeed, more than merely sound, story telling about experiences is particularly well-suited to the study of culture-in-use as well as to identity studies; precisely, what individuals experience is partially culturally constructed.

Moreover, any recounting of experience is done politically, to emphasize one aspect or another of one's world view. Poststructural and some feminist critiques of experience at first seem to threaten the soundness of experiential data by throwing into question whether individuals' knowledge of their own experiences is either individual or even representative of some reality.[1] That challenge instead thickens our understandings of both culture and subjectivity by obscuring ever further the distinction between the social and the individual. Awareness of this indistinctness of the social and the individual opens new interpretations of what it means to 'know.' Reading experience as personally, socially and politically constituted enriches our understanding of those 'experiences' and opens the door for new and less reductive kinds of meaningful analysis. Thus the poststructural/postmodern critique of experience does not spell catastrophe for interpretive researchers but, rather, points to new layers within what we call experience and more complex ways to implement these epistemologies and methodologies.

The Thickening of Experience: Language and Discourse

Experience is inherently social and cultural. Furthermore, each recounting of an experience is a political endeavor, as certain of its elements are variously highlighted and others relegated to the shadows. Before it can be political, experience is social, enmeshed in discourse, constrained by the linguistic and cultural parameters by which it can even be discerned as experience.

Putting an experience into language transforms it. Alice Jardine criticizes modern theorists for believing that 'language expresses-without-loss-of-reality, that it [language] can faithfully translate experience, that it makes no *difference*' (1993:437, original emphasis). She wisely cautions against believing that 'language is superfluous to life' (ibid.). Language, which is understood to be the basis for the social, must then be examined on a number of levels.

First, because humans think linguistically, our realities are necessarily structured by the language we use. We recognize that which we can name, or that which can be named. Conversely, that which lies outside language is seldom recognized, yet our senses perceive more than we can name. The result is an always incomplete understanding of that which surrounds us, of that which 'happens.' Clearly, we see that what is called 'experience' is in part an effect of language, a product of the linguistic framework rather than the total and unaltered perception of that which surrounds us. Some events are selected and identified as things that 'happen,' particular kinds of things in the environment are defined as being present. What is 'there' and what 'happens' are then used to explain each other, but the range of possible explanations is always already limited by and constituted through language.

Moreover, because language is social, it is one locus for the exercise of power. Power need not be construed only as a prohibitive, top-down phenomenon, but may also be viewed as a local, bottom-up exercise of both creativity and self-regulation (or yet other ways). Some ways of recognizing experience are linguistically more prone to carry authority than are others, revealing power relations within language. Think, for example, of how little authority might be commanded by those who have never been taught or who do not understand the grammatical structure of high English. Further, when language becomes normalized into discourse, power relations which are always lurking about become ever more visible. Through language and discourse, a link can be made between experience and culture. Experiential data become less distinct from cultural data.

At times, there may be a discrepancy between dominant ideologies and the experiential data of daily living (for example, see Williams, 1991; Dobash and Dobash, 1992). Take the example of wife rape. In the not-so-distant past, it was not possible for a man criminally to rape his wife. Wives could not claim that 'experience.' Some women may have perceived the unfairness of forced sex and a few may have even called it rape (after all, discursive change happens), but, by and large, wives did not identify themselves as having been raped, even if the incident was brutally violent (see Russell, 1982). As the discourse or set of discourses called feminism temporarily gained (at least some) cultural power, wife rape was re-evaluated as an event and women were able to go back and rename their experience as 'rape' *per se*. As cultural meanings change, so too do the ways we count different kinds of experiences. Moreover, the study and discussion of experience reveal much about the power relations that shape and define experiences in part through the very framework of language in which experiences are named.

Experience is not only structured through language, but is transformed into a social and cultural product.[2] It becomes the way we are constituted as particular kinds of subjects. Joan W. Scott argues this point directly when she suggests that 'It is not individuals who have experience, but subjects who are constituted through experience' (1992:26). What has been called 'experience' is, in effect, the linguistic/social and cultural frameworks within whose parameters we are constituted as subjects, within whose framework we come to self-awareness and within whose confines our consciousness lies. Scott says, 'Experience is at once always already an interpretation *and* is in need of interpretation. What counts as experience is neither self-evident nor straightforward; it is always contested, always therefore political' (ibid.: 37). In this sense, then, experience is always already social, cultural and political as well as personal.

Personal Experience and Political Meaning: Experience as Social Studies

What, then, does this conception of experience do for interpretive methodologies? Can scholars afford to give experience up as a way of knowing or learning? We argue that we cannot and should not. Experience does not escape discourse, and this is its merit. It offers an individualized window into the ways that discourse[3] operates to structure everything which comes to be called our experiences.[4] Poststructuralists have 'thickened' the notion of experience so that not only can we tap the personal, but also we get at the social. Joan Scott insightfully suggests, 'Experience is not a word we can do without . . . Given the ubiquity of the term it seems to me more useful to work with it, to analyze its operations and redefine its meaning. This entails focusing on processes of identity production, and insisting on the discursive nature of "experience" and on the politics of its construction' (1992:37). Thus experience is not only what we could *use* to do the explaining, but also *the very thing we should be explaining*.

It seems especially critical to us to continue to work with experience as data of sorts. That experience is structured through language by existing social relations is not good enough reason to abandon it altogether. Instead, scholars must interrogate experience for its contribution to the creation and maintenance of an alleged hegemony, as Ewick and Silbey (1995) suggest.

Because stories rearticulate dominant cultural norms, often in particular, personal ways, they illuminate (and create) that which is simultaneously cultural and personal. We understand experience to be a site of interaction between the individual and the cultural.

Stories, Identity and Culture

Stories, as one way to share experiences, are part of people's routine communications (see White, 1987). Because they relate experiences, stories carry information about culture, as known by the storyteller. Ewick and Silbey say, 'stories people tell about themselves and their lives both constitute and interpret those lives; the stories describe the world as it is lived and understood by the storyteller' (1995:198). Similarly, Riessman writes that 'culture "speaks itself" through an individual's story' (1993:5). It is in this sense that we use the term 'story' and it is this culture-in-use that we are attempting to capture in the snapshot form of stories told by street-level bureaucrats.

Story telling is an almost reflexive means to relate personal experiences. Catherine Riessman explains, 'A teller in a conversation takes a listener into a past time or "world" and recapitulates what happened' (ibid.:3), giving subjective order to events and experiences. Authorship of the experiences to be included or excluded belongs to the storyteller. Through stories, participants can selectively relate everyday, subjective experiences of the teller. Grounded in experience, 'narratives bridge the gap between daily social interaction and large-scale social structures' (Ewick and Silbey, 1995:198). They navigate between the particular, routine lives of the characters in the story and the broader, sociohistorical context which infuses the specifics of a story with social meaning. As they are recognized and recounted, specific everyday events are situated by the storyteller in the broader social background from which they emerge.

Because we are interested in identity, stories are particularly useful to us on two levels. First, as Riessman suggests, 'Because the approach gives prominence to human agency and imagination, it is well suited to studies of subjectivity and identity' (1993:5). Stories allow space for the richness of character that must be available to the students of identity. Through stories, participants are able to explain who they are and how that relates to the action of the story. Identities themselves are recreated through stories and story telling. Rosenwald and Ochberg astutely point out, 'Personal stories are not merely a way of telling someone (or oneself) about one's life; they are the means by which identities may be fashioned' (1992:1). Stories serve to construct the character even as the character constructs the story.

But stories also tell about identity on the social level, as a set of cultural groupings. Most broadly, Ewick and Silbey suggest that although stories can be a space of resistance to cultural tropes, they are also vehicles to teach hegemonic norms. They repeat and refract cultural expectations in ways that make shared norms personal and alive. Ewick and Silbey write, 'the structure, the content, and the performance of stories . . . often articulate and reproduce existing ideologies and hegemonic relations of power and inequality' (1995: 212). Similarly, John C. Meyer, describing the transfer of office knowledge, suggests that 'stories [reflect] the values operative in the organization' (1995: 211). Stories are able to capture identity simultaneously on subjective, social and organizational levels. A story is, indeed, a particularized representation of culture, containing elements of both the social and the individual. In this way, stories give insight into culture as it is lived, experienced and understood by the storyteller.

A Working Methodology

It was with this theoretical understanding of narrative data and experience that the methodology for this study was undertaken. Interviewing can be opened into something similar to the method for this project, but simply asking a question serves to channel the response. Although participants were interviewed at various points throughout the project, their story contributions were separate and more unrestricted.

Interviews and Stories

Despite our continued faith in interviewing as a way to learn about someone else's experiences, the technique does have (at least) one problem. Interviewing entails the researcher leading the participant to a particular experience and then drawing out details of that experience through interview questions. The data that are collected have been structured by the researcher rather than the participant, thus transforming the 'experience' once again. Moreover, the participant probably cannot recount (and has not even noticed) every detail of the experience: the researcher can never truly inter-view that experience. Rather, certain aspects of the experience are highlighted and others are forgotten or ignored. Through the interview process, the researcher reshapes the participant's experience, bringing new things to bear that the participant – to whom the experience belongs – might otherwise have left out. Other things are lost, which the owner of the experience might have deemed important, had the right question been asked.

While interviews are also excellent resources for gaining data rich with details about people's personal working knowledges, story-based research can be deployed as a tool for expanding participant input.[5] Where interview questions can presuppose answers and restrict the domain of possible responses, an invitation to tell a story presupposes that there will be some response, and does not guide the content of that response to nearly the same extent. Asking participants to tell stories rather than answer a set of questions gives more authority about the content of the data to the participant. Moreover, as we explain below, participants may even be asked to revise stories, rendering even more control over the content, not to the researcher, but to the researched.

Making Narrative Data

Clearly, the emerging methodology which we found to be most attuned to the constructedness of experience and the matter of power in knowledge production is the collection and analysis of experiential data in the form of narratives. More than merely sound, narrative methods give authority over knowledge production to the participant more effectively than many traditional methods do, precisely because they rely, in part, on the *participant*'s understanding of culture and reality. Thus story telling is particularly well-suited to the study of culture-in-use as well as identity studies.

Stories are representations of experience that we tell to ourselves and to others. Ewick and Silbey say, 'stories people tell about themselves and their lives both constitute and interpret those lives; the stories describe the world as it is lived and understood by the storyteller' (1995:198). The assumption to be made is that stories contain elements of Ewick and Silbey's 'hegemonic tales' and, as such, that they represent particular information about cultural norms. In this sense, then, 'the work is itself already a copy' (Young, 1981:5).

From Theory to Practice

As Ralph Hummel argues, 'We could do worse than study and give full credence to those who manage and work to maintain not so much public administration but public service' (1991:40). Asking participants to tell stories about things that have actually happened provided us with an intriguing mixture of both groundedness, from the non-hypothetical nature of the events described, and interpretation, a function of the telling or retelling as opposed to a simple witnessing of events. This project incorporates elements of three methods: interviews, stories and actual observation of events.

Triangulation is central to the interpretation of stories. Catherine Kohler Riessman attempts to explain how narratives might be evaluated. Because recounting is selective and constructive, she says, 'There is no reason to assume that an individual's narrative will, or should be, entirely consistent from one setting to the next...In a word, traditional notions of reliability simply do not apply to narrative studies, and validity must be reconceptualized' (1993:65). Therefore it is especially important for interpretative scholars to use other information sources and procedures, like interviews, member-checking and participant observation data, to validate and analyze narrative data.

Indeed, aside from the stories, much of our analysis relies on fieldnotes from time spent interacting with officers, counselors and supervisors in their daily routines. These fieldnotes served as a backdrop to our understandings and interpretations of the stories. We realized the importance of the informational check on the stories in particular within the police setting. Glenville officers confessed a concern that their tales of police work would not be as exciting as (they assumed) we hoped they would be. Two officers in particular had this concern and one officer rescheduled his story telling sessions at least five times (often *after* we rode along with him), with the explanation that he wanted to go back through his computer files to find sufficiently exciting stories. Even as we rode along with this officer, he expressed a concern that the ride itself would be too boring. He said that, ordinarily (had one of us not been along), he would be doing some routine visits to local apartment complexes, making a pitch for the managers to cooperate with the police in the community partnership.

However, not one of his stories was about building the community partnership. Instead, they were about this criminal or that internal political struggle. And his stories were not the only example. In short, where the stories construct police work as exciting, the triangulation revealed that daily work time is often spent filling out paperwork, waiting for something to happen, or assisting with car breakdowns and other 'unexciting' but certainly important aspects of police work. Although the stories may, indeed, have been copies of images such as that put forth by $C*O*P*S$, our readings of those stories were tempered by information gathered in the interviews and 'ride-alongs.' Thickening readings of the officer's stories, this additional information gave insight to the kinds of constructions that we perceived police to be advocating.

The Glenville police, in our experience to a greater extent than the counselors, seemed to be somewhat aware that they were creating knowledge about the police department and were particular about how they wanted to do it.[6] Again, participants themselves decided which of their experiences to share as stories, and how these should be relayed as stories. Certain events were highlighted and characters portrayed in particular ways. At the time officers shared their stories – from the first telling – they were already constructed in meaningful ways, laden with the narrator's assumptions about and viewpoints of the events, and with some events undoubtedly excluded from the story altogether.

For example, one officer whose agenda involved getting the department to hire more minorities took advantage of finding a place to speak (and someone willing to listen). He told stories about what he defined as unfair hiring practices and expressed a gratitude for our listening. He used his stories as a means to make his perspectives on the department heard, perhaps even by the ranks reading the finished research product. Another officer recognized the political implications of her story when she expressed her concern that a story might paint the department as sexist, which she said she did not want, despite her story's explicitly sexist plot.

Moreover, we were also constituted as researchers in the story telling sessions. During one meeting where we were supposed to have been passive observers, for example, an officer explicitly called one of us into a debate. The point in question was whether or not officers ought to have access to official research reports about salary and benefits that had been written about them. The command staff wanted such documents suppressed, and the officer wanted our 'expert' voices to declare officially that most research documents are public information. Again, the act of telling stories and the other inter-actions we had with the participants were all moments of mutual definition: we became 'ourselves' in contrast to each other.

Collecting the Data

Two different kinds of state workers provided the data for this study over a period of about three years. In all, 15 police officers allowed 'ride-alongs' and gave recorded interviews, and a subset of ten of them also told self-selected stories about their daily experiences at work. They talked about fairness on the street and in the station and gave us first-hand experience in this regard, letting us become part of their routine, both at PD briefings and as they worked independently on patrol.

Similarly, nine individuals who worked in various positions at a VR office confidentially shared case information, opened their office doors and welcomed observation of their staff meetings. They discussed their cases freely, pondering the best course of action to bring any particular client back into the workforce, given his or her particular physical or mental disability. All nine continued participation throughout all stages of the project, including story telling. In addition to these observational data, research participants from both lines of work were asked to complete initial and exit interviews. (See Appendices A and B, respectively, for these interview structures.) They were also asked to tell stories about fairness and unfairness at work. These data, the stories, interviews and participant observations, form the primary data sets for this analysis. Secondary sources (policy manuals, media sources and so on) were used to contextualize, cross-check and otherwise enrich the primary data. See Table 3.1, which illustrates the kinds of data employed and how they are used in this study. The triangulation was done to strengthen the methodology, as well as to promote a trust relationship between the researcher and participant. A clear effort at gaining familiarity with participants' jobs, illustrated in our ride-alongs and routine attendance at meetings, not only made our interest seem more credible to the participants and added to our systematic means of collecting data, but also gave insights into the work which became invaluable in understanding the narratives. Another important step was taken to check information and to fine-tune our understanding of events and rules that were described. Newspaper articles, organizational documents and census data were used as secondary sources to provide dimension and to formulate a clear idea of the organizational, community and spatial contexts out of which the stories emerged.

Table 3.1   Overview of data sources and uses

Mode of Data	Where Used
Newspapers	Primarily Chapter 2
US Census data	Primarily Chapter 2
Official organizational documents	Chapter 2
Participant observations/fieldnotes	Chapters 2, 5, 6
Initial interviews	Chapters 2, 5, 6
Stories	Chapters 5, 6
Exit interviews	Chapter 6

At the PD, commanding officers gave us freedom to sit in on their daily patrol briefings and asked members of three squads (groups of officers who work the same temporal shift) to give the ride alongs and to participate in the initial interviews. We did 4–8 hour ride-alongs with each of 16 officers, during which we recorded an interview session with each officer. (See Appendix A.) A subset of ten of these officers was selected to continue participation in the story telling portion of the research. Those selected to be in the subset were chosen on the basis of their self-reported identity member-ships, with the intention of diversifying the respondents. Those selected were invited to continue and were given a 'sketchbook' in which to jot notes. This consisted of a few pages of blank paper and brief descriptions of the project and instructions about story telling (see Appendix C). Each participant was offered a chance to ask questions. Appointments were made to hear and record the first story, usually for about two weeks later and usually including another 4-hour ride-along. After the first story was collected, the next session was scheduled. Sometimes, more than one story was collected at a session. All told, the data collection at the police department site took over a year.

Because it was a coherent work site, and equivalent to a large police squad in organizational size, we asked the entire RSA office to cooperate fully with all parts of the research,[7] which everyone did. Instead of ride-alongs, systematic participant observations primarily took the form of attending weekly staff meetings, which lasted from one to three hours, once a week for a period of around seven months. In addition to this, we spent some time in conversation with the office staff, just 'hanging out' and listening to them talk to each other and to us, about everything from cases to home repairs. It was rare for everyone to be in the office at the same time, because several counselors spent half their time in offices in the affiliated mental health center, ComServ. We conducted nine initial interviews, as we had done at the police department. Then each staff member was given a sketchbook and an opportunity to ask questions. Everyone agreed to continue and appointments were scheduled for a couple of weeks later to begin the story collection. We will describe the story process in more detail, after introducing the storytellers. After all the stories were told, recorded and checked over by the participant, an exit interview was conducted with each participant both at the RSA and at the police department. (Again, see Appendix B.)

Because we are using identity to frame our analysis, we will present the storytellers first as a group, broken down by subject position designators. Predictably, the police officers were white (84 per cent) and male (80 per cent). However, there were a significant number of women in the Glenville police sample (27 per cent of sample). The Glenville sites also had a high number of gay participants. Nearly 17 per cent of our participants were open about this identity, with others ambiguously seeming to imply they were also gay. Most participants were married and their authority levels within their respective organizations varied. About one-quarter of the participating disability workers were living with disabilities.

The final result is nearly 50 stories which tell about participants' daily lives at work, both in the office relating with co-workers and superiors and also in their relationships with clients. The storytellers had the fullest authority in creating these stories. Except in order to focus participants on fairness issues at work and on the streets, the content of the stories was left to the discretion of the storyteller. (Again, see Appendix C.) These participant-approved, written stories are the primary data set for this analysis, with supplementary data from the interviews and fieldnotes.

For part of the initial interview, participants were asked about how they saw their own identities. As one of the central orientations of this research, the self-reported identity memberships of participants were an important consideration. Of those who completed initial interviews, some were asked to continue participation and become storytellers. In the Glenville RSA, everyone who did an initial interview also became a storyteller and there was no need to exclude anyone.[8] At the Glenville PD, of the 16 who did initial interviews and ride-alongs, a subset of ten storytellers was selected with the intention of maximizing identity diversity, in terms of group memberships such as gender, race, ethnicity, sexual orientation and so forth. One Glenville police officer did not finish because he retired and one counselor's transcripts were lost owing to technical problems. Aside from these two, everyone who became a storyteller also completed the exit interview.

Handling the Raw Data

Transcripts were created and were manipulated from their original (largely one-sided) dialogue into a written narrative. Transformations to the story were carefully considered.[9] Particularly because of the way that the stories were solicited, with participants having several days to plan and even write down a story to tell (among other reasons), we view the stories as constructed representations. We took the verbiage of the transcript, which at points contained dialogue, and transformed it into a written story. This allowed the additional information gained during follow-up probes to be inserted at logical points in the story.

Transcriptions of the oral versions of the stories were altered to fit a written genre with the approval and often the immediate assistance of the storytellers. Largely, this consisted of eliminating some of the repetition which is part of oral communication, but does not read well as written narrative. Specifically, partial sentences were deleted or completed. A good deal of repetition was removed, along with the 'ums' and 'uhs.' At times, passages of text were moved to produce temporal sequencing. The other main manipulation was to integrate responses to probes asked at the end of the session into some logical point in the narrative. Such manipulations by the research team did change the story. Simply moving from an oral to a written tradition changes the story. We do not believe that the researchers should have full authorial license to manipulate the stories, yet it seemed imperative to bring the data into a grammatical form which could then be shared on paper. What was constructed as an oral representation was reconstructed as a written text.

This reconstruction was subject to the storyteller's final approval, through a simple member-checking procedure. All participants knew that they would have final authority over the story content and they were given texts, pens and time to edit. And edit they did. Once the story was coherent as a narrative, it was returned to the storyteller for any corrections he or she might have and any clarifications to the story were addressed at that time. All changes from this session were applied to the story and the result of this process is what we counted as story data. Again, participants retained control over their texts. After the stories were made into written texts, officers and counselors reviewed them with the understanding that they were to change anything that was inaccurate or inappropriate. Any and all changes they made were incorporated into their texts.

Plans for Analysis,

In the stories that have been collected, claims about what is 'right' emerged from the analysis, reflecting a complex relationship between identity, morality and power. We use a grounded theory approach, in which we move back and forth between the data and relevant literature to explore the interconnected-ness of morality, identity and power. The stories were systematically coded according to major content items relating to the workers, clients and decisions within them. (See the Codebook in Appendix D.) The content items are derived from a grounded theory approach.

Because the relationship between identity, morality, power and action is a complex one, we do not anticipate being able, nor would we wish, to delineate clear and precise causal relationships between any of these. Rather, our intention in this analysis is to be able to describe more completely the intercon-nectedness of identity, morality and reported action. Any effort to determine with clarity the precise impact of one concept on another (or any attempt to read this text as such an effort) is misguided. Instead, we simply want to be able to describe the tight bundling of these orientations in the stories and interviews, as they are presented, sometimes clearly, and at other times ambiguously.

Notes

1   Experience, for obvious reasons, has long claimed a special place within many feminist epistemologies. Sandra Harding suggests that there is good reason to study women's experience, to treat it as scientific data: 'Knowledge...is supposed to be grounded in experience...The experiences arising from the activities assigned to women, understood through feminist theory, provide a starting point' (1990:95). If knowledge is grounded in experience, as Harding and many other feminist scholars suggest (see Nancy Hartsock, 1990: 158; Greg Sarris, 1992; and Dobash and Dobash, 1992, generally), experience as a

source of knowing necessarily assumes a trustedness, a very special authority within an interpretive research imagination. For modernist writers, experience becomes our connection to the Real, that which is objective and outside discourse. Maria Mies suggests that, 'If we [women] do not want to consent to our own scientific nonbeing, then we must have a basis upon which we can stand, from which we can be sure of reality, and from which we can judge theories opposed to our own. To begin with, that basis is none other than subjective experience' (1991:66). The dilemma is clear: experience has been a major force in asserting discursive change, but its legitimacy as a means to know reality is coming under fire from poststructuralists who deny that experience is either purely subjective or objective.

2   We do not wish to reify the notion of culture. We recognize that culture is contingent and fluid. It is a set of meanings and practices that are dependent on time and place, contingent and always partial.

3   Goldberg (1993b:57) writes, 'Discourses are the intermediary between self and society; they mediate the self as social subject.' Like Goldberg, we believe that discourses set ranges of meanings and define the parameters of what is, what can be and what can be named.

4   Some feminists argue that using experience as data will always be a conservative practice. Scott argues that 'the evidence of experience...reproduces rather than contests given ideological systems' (1992:25). Using experience as data seems not to be the way to undo the status quo, but rather to reiterate it. Jane Gallup asserts, 'The politics of experience is inevitably a conservative politics for it cannot help but conserve traditional ideological constructs which are not recognized as such but are taken for the "real"' (1983:83). Thus feminists are cautioned: one of the fundamental elements in a feminist imagination is under attack for being traitorously faithful to a hegemonic order which excludes and oppresses women. This warning seems to apply to the study of all marginal groups, unless hegemony and social order *themselves* are the topic of study.

5   Interviews and stories are different from each other, but they share some characteristics, such as a potentially open response from participants (as a grand tour interview question would have), or a chance for the participant to assume more control over the response than the researcher might have (as could happen in an active interview). We do not think that interviews and narratives are the same, but we would not want to be the ones to draw a clear line between them.

6   Perhaps this is related to the police officers being studied more often than the counselors?

7   One woman, who was the employment specialist, spent most of her time away from the office, so she was not included.

8   However, one counselor's shyness and soft-spokenness made her tapes too difficult to transcribe and her stories are not included in the analysis.

9   By contrast, see John C. Meyer's article (1995), in which interviews were analyzed. Again, one drawback to using the interviews and determining which pieces within them are to be called stories is that the power to determine lies with the researcher. Transforming the interviews into written stories and asking participants to review them serves as a check on the researchers' creation of data. Although initially it seems counter-intuitive, we believe that transforming the stories into a written tradition and giving full control over what counts as a story to the participants in the end gives them more control over the data than the seemingly less obtrusive method of analyzing interviews for the story fragments that the researchers identify.

4   Identity and Morality

The concept of identity has a long theoretical history and has recently re-emerged as culturally important. Drawing on the body of theoretical work that has already been undertaken, we understand identity to be communicative, that is, something that one must convey to others. At the same time, we understand identity making to be a two-way communication process, in which one acts out one's identity, but also in which others respond and act on that identity. In this sense, the process of becoming, or of making an identity, is unending, evolving both actively and reactively sometimes in an impromptu fashion. We find the process of identification to be an ever-changing reformulation that is simultaneously the product of cultural norms, personal actions and interpersonal relations.

With the emergence of our perspective of identity, we must relate that concept to a notion of moral view and moral action as identity making. In this chapter, the reader should gain a sense of how we are using each of these terms as we analyze the stories in the coming chapters.

Literatures of Identity

One consideration that must be illuminated by identity theorists is how the individual relates to a group within any identity category. This is to pose the question, for example, 'How does any particular student relate to the category "student" in specific and revealing ways, such that the individual makes himself or herself as well as others aware that he or she belongs to the category "students?"' Although the question at first seems rather obvious, understandings about the relationship of the specific individual to the general category set the parameters for an entire framework to understand identity. To what extent does the individual have freedom to choose different memberships? To what extent are these imposed by others? How much flexibility is there within any particular category: how many ways are there to be, say, a student? When we consider that each of us has many memberships, new and perhaps even more complex questions emerge. How do we move among these identity memberships and still retain the identities that are simultaneously held? For example, when one is at home being a parent, spouse, community leader and so on, is one still a student in the same way that one is a student while studying, sitting in class and taking exams? This fluid intersection of individual action, social reaction and confluence and contradiction of multiple memberships presents the basis of our identity framework.

Facing the Self

From a psychological perspective, social identity theory (SIT) draws substantially on social theory, and assumes a boundedness between social processes and individual behavior, meaning that the individual is constrained by that reactive element which is loosely but widely shared by those in society. Hogg and Abrams write, 'People derive their identity (their sense of self, their self-concept) in great part from the social categories to which they belong' (1988:19). The relationship of the individual member to the general social category is mediated by processes of 'social identification.' Astutely, SIT scholars define social categories such as 'black/white' or 'woman/man' as historically constructed and hierarchically arranged. They tend to understand identity as inherently infused with power.

Rather than focusing on individuals in groups, SIT concentrates on the groups in the individual. Because individuals belong to many different categories, they have multiple identities upon which to draw. The sum of this repertoire of social identities specific to an individual makes each person unique. An individual interacts with social categories to develop a self-concept and to make sense of others he or she may encounter in daily life. Social identification, then, is 'that part of an individual's self-concept which derives from [one's] knowledge of membership in a social group together with the value and emotional significance attached to that membership' (Tajfel, 1978:63). The historical context in which individuals live defines the parameters and meanings of social groups, while individuals evaluate and emotively and cognitively integrate those cultural parameters and meanings into their own self-concepts.

Many social psychologists presume the power of dominant ideology to fix identities: 'individual human beings are born into this structure, and by virtue of their place of birth, skin color, parentage, physiology, and so forth, fall into some categories and not others' (Hogg and Abrams, 1988:27). This perspective focuses on individual tendencies to accentuate a particular group membership over others. 'Different times, places and circumstances render different self-identifications "salient." The self is thus both enduring and stable, and also responsive to situational or exogenous factors' (ibid., 1988: 25). Salience and strength of a social identity indicate how attached an individual is to each in the set of groups to which he or she belongs.

From the SIT perspective, a number of important ideas emerge. First, and basic to our own perspective, SIT scholars recognize that each of us has multiple group memberships. We each have more than one identity to draw upon; context influences which identity may be the most obvious, or salient, at any particular time. However, SIT scholars problematically overlook the simultaneity of plural memberships and take these multiple identities to be independent of each other. For example, Huo *et al.* (1996) state their assumption that 'identification with particular groups can be treated as independent constructs.' Also problematically, this genre of theorists assumes that there is something that exists outside identity, a self who can choose which identity is important, like selecting a jacket from the closet. Hogg and Abram write, 'The self-reflective nature of human beings entails that self is both object and subject, that there is a "me" for the "I" to reflect upon... The self is thus both enduring and stable, and also responsive to situational or exogenous factors' (Hogg and Abram, 1988:24–5).

Many who have applied SIT in their empirical work largely treat multiple group memberships as independent of each other (Huo *et al.*, 1996:6). The perspective shares an assumption that there is a core self who chooses which identity to portray, independent of other identities, in any given context. Thus actors alternate among basically unrelated 'faces,' depending on the context. For example, the same person may be bank president at work and then mother at home, wearing different 'faces' in each context, and with no interaction between the two identities. The identity selection is done by some faceless self who is outside or distinct from the identities themselves, who is able to put on first one and then another face. Such faces do not mutually define one another and it could even be possible for a given actor at times to wear no face at all.

The Interexistence of Identities: Away from the Modern Subject

Conceptually distinct from discrete, face-like notions of identities, feminist, anti-racist scholar Kimberle Crenshaw (1995) argues that our categorical identities intersect with each other to create unique, intersecting combinations. For example, a black woman's identity is not simply a black identity plus a female identity. Instead, it involves a unique set of identifications that is neither primarily black nor primarily female. Identities inter-exist, each inseparable, depending on the other and practically indistinguishable. The black woman's blackness is brought into being by her femininity and, conversely, her femininity is defined and realized in and through her blackness. This is the complexity of identity. Moreover, many cultural theorists reject the idea that an unidentified self exists outside the discourses through which we are identified. In other words, there is no one to 'choose faces' because the only one who exists does so in and through the very identity categories it is said to be outside. Thus we are always already identified through discourse and language.

Language and Identity

Robert Young's interpretation of Saussure suggests that "'in language there are only differences *without positive terms*'" (Saussure, cited in Young, 1981: 2). Thus, for example, the signifier 'woman' can never be reduced to some objectively real 'woman': the essence of womanhood, the standard through which all women can be recognized and understood. There is no such positive term, no such center, but only an endless and endlessly transforming set of negative terms: woman is not x, not y, not z, and so forth. Even the positive term itself, the signifier, suggests Derrida, is always only a substitute, and fails to substitute itself for anything real: 'The substitute does not substitute itself for anything which has somehow existed before it' (Derrida, 1978:280). The process of signification is itself a displacement of the signified. The word is not the object, nor is there one object that can wholly capture what is meant by the term. There is only representation. As Derrida has suggested, there can never be any literal meaning. This approach to understanding language and culture has the capacity to account for the potential to transform existential and material conditions, as it introduces a freedom for individual subjects to take up any identity, 'woman' for example, in an endlessly transforming array of possible performances, as Butler points out (1990).

Towards a More Adequate Notion of Identity

It becomes clear from the discussion above that we accept Lacan's notion of subjectivity as something structured like a language (see Young, 1981:13). Identity categories can be nothing other than signifiers which are not attached to any Real signified, and the invocation of such a category marks a displacement from the signified. These identity categories, then, are indeed analogous to language utterances: their articulation (and, by extension, their coming into being) is always already structured through discourse as language is structured by words and by grammar. As words have meaning before one utters them, so does an identity have a shared meaning before one can *be* that identity.

Moreover, there is play or slippage between the articulation/performance and its interpretation, just as there is play between the connotative and denotative meanings of the uttered/written word. Thus we understand Derrida's assertion that 'Play is the disruption of presence' (Derrida, 1978: 292) to mean that transcendental presence is made impossible by the endless and groundless movement, or play, within the process of signification. Judith Butler (1995) points to a relationship of mutual definition between identified subjects and the identity categories they claim or that claim them. Neither one can fully represent the other: the category is not the thing and the thing is not every member of the category. Thus, there is play, in Derrida's sense, between any particular woman's way of being female and the broader discourses of femininity.

Not entirely different from this, Althusser suggests that individuals are hailed or interpellated by ideological apparatuses which serve state legitimacy. The making of an individual into a subject is revealed through an oversimplified drama analogy. A symbolic character, Ideology, calls, 'Hey you, there!' Willingly, but without choice, recognizing herself in the 'you' or the hailing, the other symbolic character, the Subject, turns around asking, 'Who me?' and in the process has been made a subject (again). (Althusser, in Brewster, 1991:163). As ideology hails us, we, (mis)recognizing ourselves in the hailing, respond by willingly accepting what we think we recognize: an identified subject. Althusser writes that, by responding to the hailing, 'he becomes a *subject*. Why? Because he has recognized that the hail was "really" addressed to him, and that "it was *really him* who was hailed" (and not someone else)' (ibid.). For Althusser, these ideologies serve the state. The creation of identified subjects is a means of social control, a way for the state to perpetuate itself.

Althusser suggests that the term 'subject' itself means 'a subjected being, who submits to a higher authority, and is therefore stripped of all freedom except that of freely accepting his submission' (ibid.:169). For Althusser, there is an unmasked intention for social control. Interpellation is nothing other than a means to ensure that subjects remain well within the confines of, in particular, the state ideology. For Foucault, too, social control is the driving force. He says technologies of power are 'the new techniques by which the individual could be integrated into the social entity' (Foucault, 1988:153). Thus combining these two theorists produces a notion of subjects created and identified by the state for its own legitimation and perpetuation. On this level, then, identity becomes a matter of social control.

Identifiable Selves

Of course, identity is not *only* a matter of social control, but a matter of sociality itself. We have come to argue that identity is a given actor's composite of her or his many subject positions (Mouffe, 1995:33). Thus we are never only women or men, nor are we only members of a race or nation or profession. These intersect, mutually defining the way each subject position becomes part of the whole at any particular moment. The ways in which one is female depend on her racial, national and/or professional positionings, and vice versa. Multiple subject positions which combine to create an identity thus do not co-exist, but inter-exist. They are not separate entities, but rather determine each other in a constant process of 'subversion and overdetermination' (ibid.:34). Each centerless term defines others in a ceaseless, situational process.

The same subject position might be taken up one way by one agent and a different way by a different agent, perhaps depending on which other subject positions are involved, because identity is interactive. It may even be taken up differently by the same subject at different times because identities are fluid, dynamic and contextually oriented. People who relate to each other on the basis of one identification in one situation certainly cannot always be expected to relate to others in a different situation on the basis of the same identification because identity is dynamic. Instead, context, in terms of social relations, events and also space itself, makes certain identities more directly germaine and others relevant only indirectly.

Each subject position is both laden with social meaning and yet also taken up subjectively (Laclau and Zac, 1994).[1] Each of us belongs to many social groups, including but not limited to races, ethnicities, sexes, genders, occupations and families (see Young, 1990; Walzer, 1983). These attributes take their meanings through social expectations; thus we as a social body know roughly what it means to be, for example, 'masculine' or 'teacher-like.' We recognize these relatively stable attributes in others and can therefore identify others as 'men' or 'teachers,' to extend the example. Joan Scott puts it this way: 'identity is taken as the referential sign of a fixed set of customs, practices, and meanings, an enduring heritage, a readily identifiable sociological category, a set of shared traits and/or experiences' (Scott, 1995:5).

These social expectations, though varied, inform social relations, often from the inside out, as we re-cognize our particular understandings of these expectations in ourselves as well, *becoming* the attributes we find ourselves to be (see Hall, 1996:4). In other words, we find ourselves to be some identity, such as female, and we apply some of our own particular socially-learned ideas about what it is to be female. These are brought to life in and through our other identities (middle-class, adult, heterosexual and so on) and the social expectations of these other identities as well. Sifting through those sometimes conflicting social meanings, we take up identity subjectively, making it our own, making it our-self.[2] This is the on-going process of identity making. It is always already under way; social relations are under constant (re)definition (see Butler, 1992).

Identities, Roles and Memberships

Identities can be distinguished from roles in our account simply by reflecting on the assumptions each term seems to be making about a self. As we have already suggested, one problem with some identity theory is its implicit insistence on a self who selects which identities or 'roles' to highlight in a particular context. Although in comparing the list of things that might be 'roles' with the list of things that we might call 'identity' we find considerable overlap (worker, mother, student, husband and so on), we think that we can do away with the term 'roles' for its implied commitment to a modern, volitional subject. For example, because being a worker is not separable from being a man or a parent, in our experience, we find that these subject positions inter-exist: that is, they define and create each other. Moreover, there is no self who chooses when to be 'father' and when to be 'worker.' The two operate together all the time, though in fluctuating degrees, as context demands. Thus, for maintaining the two important assumptions we wish to avoid, independence of subject positions and a rational self who chooses among them, we find the term 'role' to be incongruous with our conception of identity and therefore do not use it.

There is also some debate about which group memberships should count as identities. For example, if one is a born-again Christian, is that an identity or a simple membership? Some kinds of group membership are ones of which we find ourselves always already members, such as of a sex, a race or a class. Iris Young reserves the term 'social group' for these kinds of memberships, and she is specifically referring to memberships into which we are thrown, rather than those which we have chosen. She writes, 'one *finds oneself* as a member of a group, which one experiences as always already having been. For our identities are defined in relation to how others identify us' (1990:46). These 'thrown' group memberships are not static, but change throughout a lifetime. As we age, we are thrown into different age memberships. An actor may realize, after years of heterosexual practice, that he or she is gay. In Young's perspective, this is not a matter of choice, but of discovery: one finds oneself thrown into a new sexual orientation.

What is excluded from Young's identity perspective is memberships in what she calls 'associations.' She writes, 'A person joins an association, and even if membership in it fundamentally affects one's life, one does not take that membership to define one's very identity in the way, for example, being Navaho might' (ibid.). We suspect that, for Young, being a born-again Christian is not an identity, but an association membership. Other affiliations, too, might escape her definition of identity, such as political affiliation, occupation and perhaps even such basic identifying attributes as marital status or parental status. It is here that our conception of identity departs from Young's.

Michael Walzer conceives of identity more broadly than Young, as he includes both the memberships into which we are born, such as citizenship status, and also those we choose to become, such as 'police officer' or (we suspect) a born-again Christian, to exhaust the example (1983:31–2). We find the inclusiveness of Walzer's definition appealing, as it can offer one account of the social mobility (in a cultural rather than class-bound sense) that allows for identities to be fluid. Including some associative memberships as identities and examining various group memberships simultaneously permits an understanding of identity as fluid and of individuals as mobile.

However, Walzer's scheme is not explicit about the differences between kinds of membership, chosen or thrown. Clearly, there is an issue of power which must be addressed by a fully useable account of identity. If, for example, a Democrat becomes dissatisfied with membership in the party and with the reputation that accompanies such membership, he or she can simply choose again and become, say, a member of the Socialist Party. However, if a Navaho person becomes similarly dissatisfied, he or she cannot simply become Asian American. Thus, although we argue that identity is about more than simply what we determine ourselves to be, still those memberships that we choose[3] ought not to be ignored.

Theorist Frederick Samuels charts various groups along two axes to gauge the depth of membership. The first of these axes is the duration of membership. Some groups are extremely short-lived, like a study group or a summer sports team. Others are much longer, but still finite, like a marital or consanguine family. Some others are in the middle, like occupation, political party or religion. Some social groups are what Samuels calls durable: these are the longest-lived groups such as race and sex (Samuels, 1977:9–10).

The second axis is the ease with which individual members can leave the group. He suggests that it is easier to withdraw from some groups, such as occupation or political party, than it is to withdraw from others, such as sex, race or ethnicity (ibid.:11). (Interestingly, social class is in the middle of Samuels' member permanence axis.) Combining these two axes, we find that sex, race and ethnic background are the most durable memberships, but that religion, political party, citizenship and occupation are also important and durable. Using these two axes, we have a framework, albeit rough, for thinking about the stability of some identities versus others.

A final point about Samuels' conception is that some memberships are neither durable nor difficult to quit. These memberships are not identities. However, it is not possible to delineate clearly where that boundary lies. Even in our discussions as we drew an arbitrary boundary, a contradiction would invariably arise, demanding that we reconsider. The distinction between simple memberships and identities is fluid and perhaps even contradictory. The usefulness of Samuels' tool lies not in what it excludes, but in how it weighs the various memberships that it includes.

The Difference Identities Make

We have argued that the relevance of identity is central. Who we are tells us and others alike how to behave and what to expect in social interaction. Of the basic importance of identity, Zygmunt Bauman writes, 'One thinks of identity ...so that both sides would know how to go on in each other's presence' (Bauman, 1996:19). Identity, although unstable and contradictory, informs the basis of social relations in a ceaseless process of negotiation.

To illustrate how these theoretical dynamics are scripted in the everyday, we offer a story told by a Glenville officer as he negotiates the daily decisions of his job. The identity dynamics are explicit and foregrounded.

> *I got a call for a criminal damage report. Well, it was a dispute between two neighbors...So when I got there, I noticed that the front door had lipstick written on it and in real big letters it said, 'I know you have my coat and my stereo. You better give it back.' It was the size of the whole front door in real dark red lipstick. So I contacted the girl that lived there. She was a white female student whose parents were from the area. She was in her early 20s, nice looking girl, you know, typical college. 'Yeah, my neighbor...she had her stereo stolen and she had her jacket stolen and now she thinks we did it...We know she's the one who wrote on the lipstick because she's left messages on our machine saying, "I know you have my coat and my stereo...You better give it back...."'*
>
> *So, basically I had a criminal damage and I could've easily arrested, but...she agreed and the victim agreed that once they leave that evening, she would clean the door and all that and then she agreed to give the victim $30 right there while we was there...I don't think on another day I would have arrested in this scenario, but in a lot of criminal damage cases like that, the normal routine would be just to arrest the person...I'd have to put a little more thought into the decision had the suspect been male, because physically he'd be more capable of hurting someone there. But, as long as, you know, he didn't seem insane, it didn't seem like there was no threat of violence. I guess I probably would put more thought into the fact that he's male.[4]*

Our point is simple: identity matters in a definitional way. In this case, cultural representations about women and femininity are conjoined with the action taken by the officer, who represents the state. In the officer's rendition, identity defined the situation, its characters and the action plot. The officer's common sense about what course of action he ought to take was closely related to matters of identity. The 'ought' of morality becomes a factor in action and identity.

Identity and Morality: Gilligan to Goldberg

Questions of identity and moral decisions have largely been limited to studying the ways in which, specifically, gender socialization shapes moral decision making. Carol Gilligan opened this conversation with her critique of Lawrence Kohlberg's theory of moral development. Kohlberg presented participants with a hypothetical dilemma[5] and, on the basis of their justifications for resolutions, offered a theory of moral development. Kohlberg found a gender difference in adult responses, suggesting the women were less likely than men to achieve the final stages of moral development (Meyers and Kittay, 1987:6).

In response to this finding, Gilligan (1982) argues that her work reveals two, equally valid, tracks of moral thinking which she links to gender difference. At the center of one track – known to us through Kohlberg – is justice, operating as a universal and abstract principle. Marilyn Freidman argues that, for Kohlberg's justice track, 'moral orientation is treated not as expressing the interpretation of situational fact, but rather as the expression of universalizable "ought" claims' (1987:194). Thus an abstract set of moral principles which applies universally is likely to reveal an orientation towards morality-as-justice. This is the orientation that Kohlberg deemed 'mature' and found in men more often than in women.

Driving the other track is a relational, contextual notion: care. Seyla Benhabib describes it this way: 'In this second set, the care orientation, moral problems arise from conflicting responsibilities to particular, dependent others; moral development requires the increased capacity for understanding and care... and such resolutions should be arrived at through the contextual and inductive thinking characteristic of taking the role of the particular other' (Benhabib, 1987:297). Moral thinking, Gilligan argues, generally incorporates elements of both, but men tend more heavily towards the justice track, while women more often employ the care track. The difference is neither completely gender-driven nor biological (Gilligan, 1986:327). Her work has had mixed reactions, sparking a debate that is at once philosophical and methodological.

Philosophically,[6] Gilligan's proposition has met resistance from some groups of feminists. Linda Kerber (1986) argues that introducing two distinguishable tracks of morality is dangerously close to the doctrine of 'separate spheres.' She comments, 'Gilligan is invigorating in her insistence that behavior once denigrated as waffling, indecisive, and demeaningly "effeminate" ought rather to be valued as complex, constructive, and humane. Yet this historian, at least, is haunted by the sense that we have heard this argument before, vested in different language... Central to the traditions of our culture has been the ascription of reason to men and feeling to women' (1986:306). Kerber points to one of the pitfalls of feminist theories rooted in difference. It is rather simple to separate the sexes, but the problem arises that, once such distinctions are made, they are often used as the basis for devaluing the experiences of women. In this case, morality-as-justice is valued over morality-as-care (Freidman, 1987:194).

Research has done little to dissolve the juxtaposition of the two moral orientations and its underlying gender distinction. Lawrence Walker (1984) compared 19 studies of gender and moral decision making against each other and found very little evidence of gender difference among them.[7] Yet others insist that there is such a difference (Stiller and Forrest, 1990; Krebs *et al.*, 1994; Tetenbaum and Pearson, 1989). More specifically, some have found that, while there may be a gender difference, other differences, such as age and class, in particular, account for a great deal more of the variation than gender does (Thoma, 1986; Kerber, 1986). And so the debate rages, expanding recently to include some consideration of how race might enter the discussion (Harding, 1987).

Much of this research makes a problematic assumption about identity. No identity category (not gender, not class and not race) operates in a vacuum. Instead, the various subject positions that one occupies (that is, female, Latina, middle class) combine and integrate, flux and flow, in different ways at different times. We argue that it may be this complexity of identity that confounds research regarding identity and moral decisions, much of which has unproblematically isolated a particular identity category through which to study moral difference. The oversimplification of identity does not allow, then, for differences within identity categories. Thus the 'gender difference' appears confusing, ambiguous or vague. The model of single identity categories driving moral decision making is reductionist and too simple to adequately reveal the relationship between identity and moral decisions.

Rather than attempting to continue the arguments about whether or not particular subject positions (for example, woman/man) drive moral thinking, several innovative theorists have offered a slightly more flexible understanding of the different moral orientations. Conley and O'Barr, for instance, assert that 'the distribution of the rule and relational orientations appears to parallel the distribution of powerful and powerless speech styles' (1990:80). Thus it is not gender (or race, or class and so on) which determines morality, but rather, one's position within social hierarchies, in this case identified by speech style.

The most complex perspective emerges in the writings of Zygmunt Bauman (1993) and David Goldberg (1993a). Rather than focusing on the ways that morality is driven by identity, these two theorists, in particular, focus instead on the overlap between identity and morality, defining each as irrevocably interwoven with the other. Bauman begins by contrasting his own perspective on morality to what he outlines as a modernist approach. He argues that modernist notions of morality rest on universality, among other things. By contrast, his understanding of morality is such that it 'may be only *heteronomous*' (1993:62, original emphasis). He acknowledges that there is more than one 'right way' and that, in fact, the same decision or act can be at once right and wrong. His enriched concept of morality accounts for a greater level of complexity and destroys the modernist notion that some universal law of morality may be uncovered. He writes, 'the long and earnest efforts of modernity have been misguided, undertaken under false pretenses and bound to – sooner or later – run their course . . . The foolproof–universal and unshakeably founded – ethical code will never be found' perhaps because such a moral code is a contradiction in terms (ibid.:10). Yet, for Bauman, the rejection of universal rights and wrongs does not absolve us of moral responsibility. Indeed, he suggests the contrary.

Instead of an abstract ethical code to which humans must submit, Bauman defines morality as a responsibility to others. Moreover, the recognition of such responsibility marks a moment of self-constitution. A self comes into conscious being in part through a recognition of moral responsibility to others. Bauman writes, 'The awakening is not in the "I am I," but in the "I am *for*." . . . Awakening to being for the Other is the awakening of the self, which is the birth of the self . . . It is such responsibility . . . that makes me into I' (ibid.: 76–7, original emphasis). The birth of a self coincides exactly with the birth of morality. Each constitutes the other initially and ever after.[8]

Moreover, like the subject position which becomes identity, the responsibility to the Other is experienced as always already assumed. Rather than choosing to be responsible to some Other, that responsibility is experienced as always already 'mine.' Also like the process of identification, in which an actor struggles to take on a given subject position in particular ways, Bauman writes that the ways individual actors assume the responsibility to the Other is what defines his or her uniqueness. He writes, 'The self may be born only out of union. It is through stretching myself towards the Other that I have become the unique, the only, the irreplaceable self that I am' (ibid.:77).

Morality is bound to identity not only in this way (how the self understands its own position relative to others) but also on an interactive level, driving, in part, how social characters perceive others relative to themselves. David Goldberg argues that 'moral notions . . . are crucial in defining the interactive ways social subjects see others and conceive of themselves' (1993a). He continues, 'a central part of the order of such [social] relations is the perceived need for subjects to give account of their actions . . . Morality is the scene of this legitimation and justification' (ibid.:197). Thus morality is bound to a sense of self, helps determine our sense of others, and then becomes the grounds to legitimate who 'I' am, who I think 'you' are and how 'we' should go on. This kind of justification is important to actors, as each moral self is its own interpreter and, according to Bauman, can never be sure of its own interpretation. He writes, '*The moral self is always haunted by the suspicion that it is not moral enough'* (1993:80, original emphasis). Telling moral stories may be a second act of identity making in that the actor justifies her or his actions (which were the first acts of identity making), seeking reassurance that she or he was moral enough by acting that way.

In the next chapter, we will begin to explore the stories with these understandings of identity and morality. We want to accentuate the importance of daily acts of identification, each act bringing us closer to some desired identity or farther from an unwanted one, in ways which may or may not have been intended. Moral decisions themselves are acts of identification, each decision – and the legitimation for that decision – subtly informing social relations between actors. Such social relations are always already tainted by the traces of power, with some actors assuming more power than others in any given interaction. This combination of identity, power as the right-to-be-right, and moral justification frame and guide our interpretation of the narratives told to us by state workers.

Notes

1   Subjects are constituted in and through discourse. The slippage involved in the process of signification – of being made a subject through discourse – implies an infinite number of ways to perform precisely that subjectivity as it is discursively (re)constituted.

2   To clarify, we do not share the SIT theorists' assumption that a faceless self outside discourse is able to take up these identities in their particular ways. Rather, the uniqueness with which one takes up any given identity is a product of a unique combination of subject positions and experiences that are brought to bear on each individual – *as the individual*.

3   Again, we are not suggesting that some modernist self does this choosing but, nonetheless, something that appears as agency is involved in negotiating identity. The subject is produced discursively (see Goldberg, 1993b:56). The effect of this process often appears, in retrospect, as agency – as a voluntary choice, in part because new memberships are drawn into the fray (such as a professional identity). This is not choice in any modern sense of the word, but involves change nonetheless – discursively produced and socially enacted. Change, then, including the 'selection' of new identity memberships, is a product of the specific and unique combination of intersecting discourses which serve to constitute any given subject, as well as the individual's lifetime of experiences with and knowledge of those discourses.

4   Italics indicate passages replicated verbatim from the transformed stories told to us by officers.

5   The Heinz dilemma is as follows:

> In Europe, a woman was near death from cancer. One drug might save her, a form of radium that a druggist in the same town had recently discovered. The druggist was charging $2000, ten times what the drug cost him to make. The sick woman's husband, Heinz, went to everyone he knew to borrow the money, but he could only get together about half of what it cost. He told the druggist that his wife was dying and asked him to sell it cheaper or let him pay later. But the druggist said, 'No.' The husband got desperate and broke into the man's store to steal the drug for his wife. Should the husband have done that? Why? (Kohlberg, 1969:379).

6 We are concerned here only with the impact on philosophies of women/humanity. Owing to space constraints, we will not discuss the implications of Gilligan's work for the meaning of morality or ethics more generally. This is a somewhat distinct issue, of which Hepburn (1993) writes a rather interesting analysis.

7 Of these studies, 14 found no sex differences and five found men ahead in moral reasoning. (See Luria, 1986, for a summary.)

8 Although we think the above is Bauman's point, in all fairness, he actually offers the following irregularity between ontological and ethical being, and assigns priority to the ontological. On page 74 he insists, 'Morality is the *absolute beginning*' (original emphasis) but later he writes, 'being is before morality; the *moral* self can be no other than a moral *self*' (Bauman, 1993:74–5). While this distinction has philosophical merit, the underlying point is that morality and self-constitution are so deeply interrelated as to be only rhetorically separable.

5 Power in Motion: Negotiating the State

State agents' work is riddled with moral decision making. Street-level workers act on citizens with a right to be right, as revealed in the stories that state actors told us. Our story about the line workers' stories has two intertwined subplots. First, identity was a major factor in the stories that officers told. Many decisions can be read as moments of identification, with decisions and identity acts too closely bound to unravel. The stories reveal that moral decisions are identity decisions: that the discourses of morality are interlaced with the discourses of identity and that these discourses set the cultural parameters for justifications for authoritative acts, including the parameters for who may count as the 'authority.' Simultaneously, moral decisions are one avenue for claiming (or rejecting) an identity for one's self.

The second layer of our story line involves the re-presentation of moral decisions. That is, when participants told their stories, they recreated the scene of the moral decisions in important and telling ways. As 'the researchers,' we became characters in the moral story being told. As the listener to the stories, we became the audience to be persuaded. We were invited to be players in the moral judging taking place within and about the stories. The telling, by itself, is a second act of identification, one that is interactive and intended to be persuasive.

Before we begin to weave together our story about identity, morality and power, we should be clear that traces of Kohlberg's and Gilligan's ethics of justice and of care were very accessible from the stories. One officer, Ray Carillo, whose canine partner was killed in action, and whose story appears in more depth later in the chapter, reveals the more commonly female ethic of care. His questioning of the decision to place the dog in danger centered on factors such as *how important this dog was to me, how close we really were, how much of a friendship I had with the dog... He was important to me personally, and I was really proud of him, and the personal relationship I had with him and the companionship.* Thus the ethic of care operates at the level of (presentations of) actual decisions in the stories.

Similarly, the ethic of justice is revealed in this sergeant's story of destroying evidence to protect the reputation of a fireman.

> *It looked like a plain suicide, which is really all that it was. Tragic suicide, but really nothing more complicated than that. They had to go through his property and other things, his dresser and things of that effect to look for any suicide notes or anything that may have foretold what was to happen. As he was doing this, in a pair of the fireman's socks, he found a small vial of cocaine and instead of turning it over to the wife or letting the family know about it or anything to that effect, he just got a hold of the prosecutor and they decided just to get rid of it and be done with it and throw it away, which is exactly what happened. And here was a case where you really could have turned that thing into a big mess and said, 'Look, we've got a Glenville fireman who may have used cocaine or who may have been doing cocaine,' but instead of doing that, he got rid of it. Further investigation... revealed nothing as to any kind of widespread use.*

It could clearly be argued that this officer, who we call Rick Gartner, is operating at Kohlberg's fourth stage of the development of morality-as-justice. At this stage, 'conformity is...augmented by a sense of the value of maintaining the social order and of the contribution of dutiful conduct to that order' (Meyers and Kittay, 1987:6). The officer is aware that revealing the cocaine could undermine a social order which suggests that fireman are brave, law-abiding, professional heroes. In order to best handle emergency situations, it is important to maintain this order. After all, it is not unlike a particular social order that defines his own profession. Thus the officer acted to ensure that the investigation conformed to a social order that honors, rather than defaces, uniformed state agents.

But there is a different story to be told. Indeed, morality can be described in terms of its different facets, be they caring or justice or other normative constructions. But drawing on these non-hypothetical accounts of moral decisions, we challenge the notion that identity drives moral decisions and, instead, tell a counter-story about how moral decisions are a site of identification, how morality and identity may drive each other in partial, yet active, ways. In the story above, we began to illustrate this dynamic. The officer could have made the opposite decision (to turn in the evidence to other authorities) and still have been at Kohlberg's fourth stage. A commitment to the nation's laws and to the proper handling of evidence certainly qualifies as a dutiful contribution to protect social order.

Something more complex happened, though. This is also a story about subjectifying. The officer's comment is telling: *here was a case where you really could have turned that thing into a big mess.* We might argue that finding cocaine among the private things of fireman *already* indicates a big mess, but instead the officer determined that it would not be a mess until there was public awareness. It would not be a big mess until the identity of firemen-as-professional-heroes was at risk. Thus, in making the decision that he did, the officer in this story seizes the moment to define a subject position – to subject-ify – in a way that, for the moment, suits him. The subject position 'fireman' is rearticulated in the moral decision. Identity and morality fleetingly solidify each other, not completely, but contingently, momentarily. It is this story, of the affirmation, rejection and rearticulation of identity, that we are considering.

We certainly do not mean to raise the specter of the 'fraternity' of uniformed emergency workers. Although there was a great deal of camaraderie among the officers, there were clear divisions, too. Race was important to the fabric of identity that divided some officers from others, both on the street and in-house. The matter of race inside the department was addressed very explicitly by David Wendell, an African–American officer. He told us a story that began in the earliest days of his career, 16 years ago. It is a story of trying to inject an ethic against racism into the culture of work. He began with a historical anecdote about a racist incident between himself and another officer.

> *We went to a baseball game, our squad did... And that same officer that I felt had been prejudiced was there... So at the baseball game, it was very apparent he had been drinking a lot. He was becoming very belligerent and loud. After the game, we were walking down the walkway to the parking lot and he was behind me and there was another officer from my squad walking side-by-side with me with his wife. Well, the officer walking behind me, he all of the sudden puts his arm on my right shoulder and he says to me, 'How much money do you have, nigger?' I was shocked and I turned around to see who it was and it was this other officer. I pulled my shoulder away from him and I just kept walking to my car.*

He recognized his division from the rest of the department. *I was one of two black officers working in the Glenville Police Department.* The rest of the story was a description of how this officer has tried, without much success, to lead his department to hiring a more diverse group of officers.

The story reveals clearly that identities are multiple, fluid and intersecting: officer identities can be known only through racial identities, and gendered, sexed identities, and only momentarily. We should not be surprised to find that the moments of identification within moral decisions refract and reflect that multiplicity, fluidity and interwovenness. The remainder of this chapter looks at the moral decisions of police officers and VR counselors and explores them as moments of identification and subjectification. Generally, the protagonists of the stories reveal numerous identities. Often, several of these identities were mutually reinforced in one moral decision. The officers' representations of the decisions again reflect the play of identity.

Consider this most dramatic example of moral decision making. Officer Karen Marker fatally shot an assailant. As she represents her own thoughts about her deliberation, Karen distinguishes a time that satisfies the moral requirements of her police identity, as distinct from the moral requirement of other subject positions she occupies.

> *I would have been within department policy and within my right to fire at him as a threat to me and my partner and this kid. He's advancing on us. He's not following instructions, and he's armed. I could have fired, but in my mind, I couldn't. I couldn't. Personally, I kept thinking it's not time. I don't know. I wish I could describe it... I knew that it would have been okay for me to fire. I knew I would be justified, but in my head I didn't feel like it was time yet... Finally, he walks right up to the barrel of my gun. The knives are still pointed upward. I thought, 'Oh boy.' I mean, I'm going to have to make a decision. I know in my heart I'm justified. A part of me was telling me, 'Yes, you can shoot now,' but I just didn't feel right about it...*

The officer here recognized that many of her identities will be affected by this decision, and actively worked towards a situation where the decision could fit within all moral-identity requirements. As she recreated the drama of her decision for the researcher, Karen was explicit about there being more than just her police self on the line. In the resolution, it is more than her professional subjectivity that must be comfortable with her decision.

> *When they got to the hospital, he died on the operating table. He did not make it. An unfortunate ending to the whole thing. I mean for me that is the ultimate use of discretion in this job, the judgment to fire or not fire. The department says, 'Hey, when you're threatened or someone else is threatened, deadly physical force may be used against them.' But there is also a sense of internal discretion. There's a level inside that I need to know. Geez, I'm only on this job two years. Am I going to be able to do this again, and am I going to be comfortable with what I had to do? There's no question in my mind that I was threatened, as was my partner. At the point he slashes at the both of us, that's it. There's no question. It's time, and I can live with that.*

Moreover, Officer Marker contrasts herself to others who share her identity as police officers, but are subjectively different.

> *After this happened, I mean, you get a lot of feedback about things like that. A lot of officers came up and said, 'Aw, you know' – macho male officers – 'I would have dusted him as soon as he stepped off the dock.'*
> *'Well then, that would have been your call apparently, and if that's what you can live with, that's fine. I would not have been okay with that.'*

The theme that moral decisions are heavily layered with acts of identification repeats itself in many of the stories. In the following one, the storyteller's identities as police officer and ('good') parent are involved in his decision to gather 'victims' who would allow him to make an otherwise unsolicited arrest. The arrestee was a woman the officer identified as pregnant, a prostitute and an alcoholic who, in the process of changing her shirt,

> *exposed her breasts to everyone in the parking lot. I found a couple victims that wanted to prosecute her for that, so I ended up arresting her for indecent exposure... and brought her to jail and I pretty much sweet talked her into blowing into the breathalyzer. She did and she blew a .225, which is over twice the legal limit. She said, 'Oh that's not bad. I've been cutting down since I'm pregnant.' Right after she said that, she kind of stuck her fingers down below her waistline and smiled and said, 'Oh, he's kicking. I can feel him moving around.' She was real happy about it and didn't think anything about the fact that she was drinking. She thought that she was doing good because she was cutting down. That right there caused me a lot of problems, especially because I have a seven-month-old baby. That just really bothers me. My wife didn't touch a single sip of alcohol, didn't take any medications or anything, just because she didn't want any possible thing wrong with the baby. And this one's going to grow up with a mother who doesn't even know who the father is of her unborn child and she's out here drinking up.*

This story has several layers of identity at work. Officer Hinkley uses his identity as officer to define some people as 'victims' and those people take on that identity by agreeing to a complaint. The arrestee has committed no major violation of the law, yet Hinkley goes out of his way to arrest her. Here lies an intersection of identity and morality: as the officer criminalizes her action, he does so as a 'good' parent, which is the opposite of how he identifies the woman. His desire to subjectify her bears the mark of his own subjectivity. The moral decision here plays out as an arrest, but we suggest it is an arrest that is more about differentiating between kinds of people than it is about serving and protecting citizens.

Clinton Hinkley himself re-presents the story this way, juxtaposing his wife's behavior during the pregnancy (as well as his own) to the arrestee's. He defines his situation for the researcher audience: he and his wife are 'good' parents, non-drinking and deeply concerned people who abhor such behavior as the antagonist's. By arresting, Officer Hinkley articulates an identity for himself that is different from hers, and enforces his 'good' identity through a moralizing politics of prosecution. Identity and morality become inseparable as the moral decision provisionally defines and is defined by the identities at play in the story and its telling.[1]

Claims about the 'right' outcome to these stories interest us for what they suggest about the operation of state power at its capillary points. The identities of state agents, as for other political subjects, are fractured. Race, gender, class, occupation and any number of other social orderings mix, mesh, combine and contradict each other to create a heterogeneous, fractured body of individuals bound by a shared identity as 'state agents' whose moral intentions are complex, diverse and riddled with the traces of a whole host of other identities. While traces of the Kohlberg–Gilligan debate do surface in the stories, breaking away from a simple gendered analysis explodes the parameters of dueling ethics and invites a more complicated exploration of multiple subjectivities, political moralities and power at play.

Claiming from Structural Authority

In a simple sense, claims were made presumptively and without a second thought. After all, state workers have a structural authority over non-state workers, and this cultural ordering is rearticulated each time the authority is exercised. In the case of VR counselors, the ultimate manifestation of power is whether or not to allocate funds. Clients come to the Rehabilitation Services Administration asking for money and training to become more productive members of the workforce. However, there is a great variety in the extent and type of assistance that can be provided. In one case, a counselor, Jane (who was the office supervisor by the time she told this story), allocated RSA funds to help the private cause of a client.

> *Janet discovered that she had inherited $48,000 and was never told. Her daughter who lived in California was appointed conservator. Janet was upset since she had been living in boarding homes in South Big City and living on the bare minimum. She was also upset that the reason for the appointed conservator was the belief Janet was too sick and could not handle her own money...*
>
> *For assessment purposes, I completed a psychological evaluation at the beginning of our working together. Janet obtained a lawyer who was requesting a psychological evaluation which Janet could not afford. I believed it was in Janet's best interest to get a new evaluation rather than using one that was a couple of years old, especially in light of her obvious improvement. Although assisting with a second psych. eval. did not appear to be directly related to Janet's vocational plan, I found the process of proving competency in order to get her inheritance was causing her a great deal of stress, thereby affecting her employment...*
>
> *The results of the second psychological evaluation were very favorable. Janet's functioning improved overall and her IQ level increased significantly. This, along with the steps she had made to become more independent, helped her prove competency and she was granted control of her inheritance.*

Jane used her authority over state funds to aid a client who was fighting a personal legal battle. This is the right, indeed the power, of those who can claim identities as state agents. The second psychological evaluation did not make the woman more employable; she had a stamina problem, which prevented her from working even 20 hours a week, regardless of her IQ, yet the counselor felt that the right thing to do was to assist the woman in her struggle to get her inheritance. The counselor embraced the decision holistically, wanting to account for where the woman lived and her safety. Thus, although state authority seems to operate straightforwardly – one woman had it and the other one did not – there is something slightly more complex than a simple carrying out of policy that lies beneath the practice of allocating funds and services.

Structure, Morality, Identity

Legal claims, such as articulations of discretionary allocations of state funds or decisions about whether to arrest, are interlaced with other claims that relate to identity, moral view and lived experience. These thicker claims made by state workers, evident in the stories, begin to account for differences between and within state agencies and among their workers. They suggest that state actors do not operate solely to the benefit of the state. Nor do they simply and uniformly strive to manage their own workloads. Workers also struggle to protect and assert their own moral commitments, ones that may overlap with or directly contradict formal state morality, by which we mean the morality codified as law and articulated as policy, or asserted by senior managers and lawmakers. Two stories reveal the interconnections between morality, identity and the flow of state power.

Policing Families

Karen Marker is a conscientious, white, lesbian lieutenant. She told a story about a time when her subordinate made an unusual request to use family leave time, a carefully articulated city benefit. Despite the state's explicit definition of 'family,' the lieutenant asserts her own moral sense of the 'right' thing to do.

> *These are paid days and you get three a year. The rule that allows this says that there's a list that says who this can pertain to: your spouse, immediate family members like your parents, your children, your grandparents, maybe even nieces and nephews or uncles and aunts. I can't remember now, but immediate family. It outlines those, specifically.*

The lesbian subordinate made her request clear:

> *'Well, my partner has to undergo some surgery and I want to take the day off, so I guess what I'm saying to you is I think it's the right thing for us to do that I should*

> *be afforded the same opportunities toward emergency leave for a family situation as others in this agency are allowed to do.'*

Lt. Marker accepts and legitimates the officer's longer claim about heterosexual and same-sex partnerships being fundamentally the same. She takes this perspective as morally sound, to her, a point of common sense. Even though she recognizes that her peers and superiors in the department might not agree, Karen asserts her right to be right and grants the paid leave, legitimating her choice through the unfairness (perhaps even immorality) of discrimination.

> *It's a city benefit. It would be discriminatory, basically, to not give you this under the city policy… I think this is one of those things that gets made on its face in the sense of fairness and what's right, to be doing the right thing for the right reason. Just give me the slip. I'll sign it and send it in. Anybody wants to ask any questions about it can come ask me about it. If they don't want to ask any questions, that's fine too. I don't feel like it needs to be officially decided on by committees. I don't want to put it off and if you chance it, the answer could be no.*

The characters' identities and closely linked moral views prompt the lieutenant to use her position of authority both over the other officer and over city policy to do what she thinks is right, granting the leave time. As an officer and a leader, Lt. Marker takes responsibility, protecting her subordinate, and recognizes that another lieutenant might not make the same decision. However, because of who she is – a woman, a lesbian and a lieutenant – she is able and willing to expand the city's definition of family and legitimate her own moral position. Formal state authority competes with the complex layers of identity, moral orientations and power as policy is enacted or law enforced.

At the same department, another officer uses his authority to enact an opposite politics, enforcing hegemonic moral ethics in a story too rich to be employed only once in this study. Where Lt. Marker above worked to expand notions of family, recall Officer Clinton Hinkley, who worked hard to incriminate a woman who fell outside his view of the morally acceptable. The woman was

> *a prostitute named Angela Stevens and she's 39 years old. She's a white female and she has no teeth. According to her, a black guy beat her up one time and knocked all her teeth out. And she's a chronic alcoholic and, not only that, she's pregnant.*

As outlined earlier in the chapter, the woman changed her shirt in the parking lot of a convenience store, which the officer authoritatively defined as indecent exposure. Clinton even *'found a couple of victims'* to prosecute her and arrested the woman, choosing to define the events as a crime rather than as a street woman changing her shirt where she could. He identifies the victim not as the woman, whose life is clearly harsh and probably complicated, but instead finds a few miscellaneous people who happened to be in the parking lot at the time and names them 'victims.' Law is used to rationalize and enforce Officer Hinckley's personal moral prespective.

Hinkley operates with a set of ideas that direct how he perceives what goes on around him, and then he acts on those perceptions with material consequences for others; state power is embedded in street relations and in the moral imagination of the officer. Clinton's moral identity as 'good parent' momentarily fixes a morality of parenthood to be enforced by the state. Simultaneously, it temporarily locates relatively privileged citizens as victims and a relatively powerless one is identified as a powerful threat to that fixed, enforceable moral order of good parenting. His story expands, revealing a larger moral agenda behind the arrest. Introducing his wife as a foil character to the prostitute, the officer explains that drinking while pregnant is child abuse and should be punishable by sterilization or at least incarceration.

> She blew a .225, which is over twice the legal limit... She was real happy about it and didn't think anything about the fact that she was drinking. She thought that she was doing good because she was cutting down. That right there caused me a lot of problems, especially because I have a seven-month-old baby. That just really bothers me. My wife didn't touch a single sip of alcohol, didn't take any medications or anything, just because she didn't want any possible thing wrong with the baby. And this one's going to grow up with a mother who doesn't even know who the father is of her unborn child and she's out here drinking up...
>
> The only way you can do anything about it is if they make abortions illegal. My understanding is that there is a lot of people who get home abortions and have their own ways of aborting their children. Some of which is through alcohol or drugs, so it's just a form of abortion. That way if you have prostitutes or people out there that are doing drugs or alcohol while they're pregnant, then we can force them into custody for the term of the pregnancy to keep them from abusing the baby...The only other way to help prevent this is to give all drug addicted females, or female prostitutes a hysterectomy.

Officer Hinkley uses his position of authority to enforce his moral view to the extent that he can, with rather significant consequences for the woman involved. Interestingly, this officer extends his claim, wanting more legal legitimacy and authority to enforce his own moral agenda. His common sense of families and the ideal laws surrounding them is such that women who 'choose' not to behave in the manner he identifies for 'good mothers,' regardless of their situations, should be physically controlled, either by incarceration or by sterilization. At the same time that one officer expands the meaning of family to accommodate her life and the lives of others like her, another officer constricts it to better match his own moral identity and to delegitimate a person who is not like him and his family.

Compassion and State Funds

While facing a different set of issues than the police often did, VR counselors, too, filtered decisions through matters of identity and morality, often struggling to do what they regarded as the right thing. Priorities conflicted around issues of compassion and empowerment and the competing interest in spending state funds appropriately.

One client with a history of mental illness came to a relatively new counselor, who we call Betty. The woman's problems were not so severe that she was unable to work and she even had some technical training. However, because she did not like the job she was trained for, she sought RSA funds to be trained as a massage therapist. After deliberating, asking advice and presenting the case at a staff meeting, the counselor decided not to support the plan the woman had created for herself.

> *I think even if she gets her massage certificate and she gets out there she's probably not gonna stick with it very long. Kinda like what she's done in the past. She never really sticks with anything.*
>
> *We're not, we're not really supposed to look at cost when we're deciding stuff like this, but you're always gonna have that in the back of your mind. You don't want to go out and spend five thousand of the taxpayers' money on something that you really feel that is not gonna work out. You don't want to lose taxpayer money.*

Although tax dollars were explicitly not supposed to be the deciding factor, Betty felt that the right thing to do involved weighing money in the equation. She seemed to feel obliged to spend funds judiciously. Another counselor, Benita, took the opposite approach, generously spending funds in the name of compassion, empowerment and dessert:

> *At the Psych Consultant and Voc Rehab's request, Adam had to go through vocational and psychological testing ... The results indicated that Adam had below average intelligence and his life goal to be a mechanic was probably not possible because of his functioning ability. The test indicated that Adam would not be able to grasp the skills needed to work on cars. It was also noted that with his bi-polar, his stamina and attention span were too poor to perform the job duties. As a counselor and as a person I was disappointed at the results. Adam had so much gumption and personality. I wanted him to succeed in life. Consequently, I had a difficult decision to make. I could steer Adam in another direction and refuse to pay for mechanical training and offer something more plausible for a successful closure. Or I could take a chance on Adam and help make his dream come true ...*
>
> *I decided to honor my client's aspirations and sent him for training to become a mechanic ... Both Adam and I feel that he can make it and make something of himself for himself and his family.*

Even though her vision of the right thing to do defied the authority of the vocational and psychological tests, Benita decided to allocate state funds to empower her client, legitimating his aspirations and demonstrating to him that she believed in him. Misspending tax dollars (or even the potential of setting the client up for failure) comprised a lesser wrong for her than underestimating this man.

In another story, though, this same counselor was deeply concerned about money. Benita explained that the way the VR system fitted with other governmental assistance programs could easily result in poverty, particularly for her clients, who were severely mentally ill. Many of her clients were referred from a mental health agency in the area whose first action was to get the clients on Social Security.

> *They start receiving $400–500 a month in benefits. The next step is referring a client to Voc Rehab, where the attempt is to get them reemployed, self-sufficient and off benefits. We find them an entry level job earning $5.00 an hour for 15–30 hours a week which is half the amount of their SSI.[2] We have set the client up. We tell them it's good to be self-reliant, independent and employed but, essentially, you'll be living below poverty level... If I get a client who I know is not psychologically stable or I feel they will not hold the job for any length of time, I tell them to hold off on Voc Rehab. I am not violating any direct policies but it's certainly not popular to steer a client away from becoming employed in any fashion.*

In addition to her story about spending tax dollars against the advice of other vocational and psychological experts, Benita again circumvented the spirit of RSA policy in favor of what she defined as the right course of action for (nearly) impoverished clients. In both of these cases, Benita's own view of the 'right' ending differed from what she thought the agency wanted her to do. In both cases, she ignored the expectations of the agency and authoritatively relied on her own perspective. Her identity as state agent gave her some authority to do this, and subjectified her to be more concerned with the personal situations of clients than with the fiscal situation of RSA.

Lived Experience as Grounds for Knowing How to Act in Discretionary Moments

One counselor talked at length about the way her identity helped to create the rehabilitation plans for her clients. Judy is hearing-impaired herself, and she specializes in deaf and hearing-impaired clients. Although advocating clients' freedom to communicate in the ways that are most accessible to them is not part of vocational rehabilitation, Judy's stories imply that she spent a considerable amount of her time teaching clients about communication options.

Oralism[3] is still very strong in the hearing community for the deaf community. The hearing community think they know what's best for the deaf community. They say, 'You must live in our world, therefore you must speak. Sign language is not acceptable.' And I think that's all she [the client's mother] could see. Instead of looking at communication, she looked at trying to be 'normal.' Then the school, of course, they want oralism because it's hearing people who are the administrators.

She argued that it was owing to pressure from parents, administrators and even doctors that she often found high school-aged clients with little or no ability to communicate. Judy herself was quite successful with oralism, but she also relied on sign language. She referred often to the way her parents had given her communication options, encouraging her to use sign language and, at her own pace, to become oral.

Drawing on her own personal experiences, she often adamantly contradicts what clients' parents, doctors and teachers have told them. Judy tells her clients that these other authorities are often flagrantly misguided and that clients must be able to communicate, even if that means using only sign language and never becoming oral (which some clients took to be a sign of stupidity or a 'deficit').

Anyway, I don't think Joe's mother had full access to the deaf community information. And he definitely had been left out of the deaf community. He had just recently started to learn sign language and is doing pretty well, considering the lack of access to sign language. He had depressions. It is a shame when his mother tells me that he has a deficit in him. He's 'refusing' to speak. There's a deficit in him. And really there isn't a deficit in him. I think his depression is from not being accepted. And he must think, 'I must not be worthy.' Basically, deep down inside I wanted to slap the mother silly to wake her up to her son's need.

Moreover, Judy uses her position as a state agent to teach younger clients that, if their parents and other authority figures do not teach sign language, she sees no other solution but to exclude the parents from decision making until they become more educated about 'deaf culture.'

Ideally, I would have liked to see the mother let go of her son. She does nothing but harm... You know, high school kids come in and transition into adults... Teach them about communication. Teach them about deaf pride, since he had no pride. Leave the mother completely out of the picture. Just never say good or bad to her because he's going to tell her how he feels one day. That's normal.

These claims are outside the domain of her authority as a vocational rehabilitation counselor. She makes them from the authority of her personal and cultural experience as a hearing-impaired woman. In an overall goal to make the client as independent as possible, Judy believes that she has the right, or is 'right,' to disrupt the family relationships that interfere with what she, the state agent, wants them to be. She assumes a 'right' to determine the 'right' way to raise and treat a deaf or hearing-impaired child. Her claims are re-enforced by her position as a counselor, and she is comfortable using confidentiality laws to serve her own attempts to make her young client independent, even at the cost of the current relationship with his mother. For better or worse, Judy finds her knowledge about these matters to be the 'right' knowledge, even when compared to the parents' knowledge and at the cost of a parent–child relationship.

> *He tells me he wants to be independent, doesn't want his mother involved. I respected that and did not disclose anything to his mother. Three months later, his mother called and complained to my supervisor. She demanded to have a meeting, and was upset that I did not include her in anything. At the meeting I explained that her son requested not to have his mother involved and I too, by law, respect his right to confidentiality. She called me a liar, and did not respect the legal aspects of confidentiality.*

Thus claims to know can be made straightforwardly, as a state actor acting over any other kind of citizen, but such claims are infused by moral presumptions and efforts to produce 'justice' in the workers' resolutions to routine dilemmas. These claims are also grounded in the terrain of identity and personal experience. Judy's sense of 'right' far exceeds simply finding a job for the client and stems most visibly from her identities as state agent and hearing impaired woman. She contested the mother's right to final authority by invoking notions of justice and independence for the client (which are personal, not organizational, goals). A moral orientation for deaf and hard of hearing clients momentarily solidifies in Joe's story as the counselor uses state power to disrupt what she identifies as a family relationship which 'ought to be' disrupted.

Moreover, Judy rested on the authority of her own experience as hearing-impaired to set high standards for her clients. In this story, she draws on her personal knowledge of what she calls 'deaf culture' to define her client's behavior as inappropriate:

> *I'll call this one Tom. He is deaf. He's from Africa. Born deaf, always had access to communication. He's black, and he moved to the United States ... about ten years ago ... He is definitely from a Deaf culture. His parents were rich in Africa and he always had access to languages. He had complete, full support for whatever he wanted to do and whatever language he wanted to use. If he wanted to go to deaf school, he went to deaf school. If he wanted to do oralism, he could be oral. His parents encouraged full involvement in the deaf community. They saw what*

language was best for him and just worked with him on that and let him make decisions. He's very good at that.

Tom wants everything now. He wants comprehensive services and everything done for him. And he doesn't have a job because he's black and deaf. He is qualified to work and he has certification training in electronics assembly and design. And every time he has a problem, it's because they discriminated against him. They violated his ADA rights and EEOC rights. He's always angry. And any time he makes a mistake, it's still their fault. He also filed a complaint against Metro Center for the Deaf because they told him he has an attitude problem. He really does have an attitude problem. I believe that previous counselors never confronted issues aggressively as I have ... I made him stop hiding behind Deaf culture ... According to the other counselors for the deaf, I've been the most successful person with him. Not putting up with the excuses, and he's been employed for over a year, which is pretty good for him.

The irony of this story is that this particular counselor routinely teaches clients about self-advocacy and how to be aware of special rights and how to receive services to which people living with disabilities are entitled. Her experience as a hearing-impaired woman gives her sufficient confidence in her ability to distinguish between too much anger and just the right amount of it, thus enabling her to be a bit tough on a client, even when other counselors do not share her confidence.[4]

Sometimes identities and experiences work in contradiction to state authority, producing internal contestation over who should rightfully be the final authority on particular matters. This contestation is reflected in another counselor's critique of the eligibility policy and his belief that counselors should have the authority to make the judgment. Wherever a disability can be documented, and some benefit from services can be anticipated, RSA policy demands that services be rendered. Thomas told this story about his client:

My gut feeling was that this lady's not gonna make it. I can't help this lady out with some direction. But the people who are promoting the program from VR say they want to give anybody who comes through a chance, and to basically presume eligibility. Unless I have documented evidence to the contrary that she can't benefit from services then I should make her eligible. So I did ... Now I have a client who was referred to me for a specific service that I don't know what to do with.

Although he followed policy as he was told to do, still Thomas challenges that system and advocates allocating authority to those who 'know,' those who deal with clients and have experiential knowledge from which to draw conclusions. His stories are rife with this frustration:

But it brings up a lot of issues because there's a policy about, you know, eligibility that I try to follow. I also try to give my input as my experience and what I see in the case... So, it's kind of burdensome, and it's kind of like you know, big brother watching over you. And maybe I'm jaded. You know, maybe it's just because I've been here and I feel like I know what I'm doing ... I think they should go back to letting the folks that have the experience make my line of demarcation anywhere they want.

The point is clear: knowledge claims that are driven by experience rather than policy guidelines have intrinsic value for Thomas and he feels that such practical knowledge is undervalued by the 'big brother' management. This same story emerges from the police department, where a decision made by the on-scene authority is viewed as wrong by the officer involved. Officer Ray Carillo is a dog handler, and his dog was shot and killed as a result of a decision made by a higher-ranking officer who had little or no knowledge of canine training and strengths. He insists that experience should be considered the most important basis for knowledge claims.

I guess the final decision about the dog, the canine, I believe should be left with the handler. Who else knows? Regardless that it is a live type of instrument or equipment that belongs to the city that is handled by the officer ... It should be his decision because he's supposed to be trained and be the expert on that one equipment. If he thinks there will be any chance of failure on it, he should be the one saying, 'I can't use the equipment on this.' I think it should revert back to the handler. He should have the last 'say so' on if they use the dog or not. Then, like I said, the entry team advised not to send him in then ... in this situation it didn't solve anything. We still had to go after him [the fugitive]. Two S.W.A.T. members were both shot and my dog was killed ... Like I said, whether you use the dog or not to use it should be at the discretion of the dog handler.

Ray clearly feels that his knowledge, derived from practical experience with canines, gave him the right to know when and how the dogs should be used. This is in contrast to the SWAT (Special Weapons and Tactics) team officer who was structurally authorized to give the command to use the dog, against the advice of other officers, including the dog handler himself. Officer Carillo grounds his critique in experience and insists that experience should give one the right to know.

In the final story, it is identity itself which connects an officer to a citizen so strongly that the officer flagrantly disobeys authority to give a break to a citizen whom he identifies as 'like him.' Three characters in the story have engaged in criminal activities. The other characters include the narrator, Mani Sano, who is a hard-working, Mexican–American patrol officer, and his white supervisors. Two male small-time marijuana dealers team up to rob their supplier, who believes himself to be their friend. While one waits in the getaway car, the other enters the house and prepares to shoot the supplier, who is a Mexican man supporting his extended family. In a rapid turn of events, the supplier takes the gun from the intruder and fires at him as he flees the house to the awaiting car. Officer Sano relates to the Mexican man as he narrates, telling his audience about how hard Francisco works to support not only his wife, but his brother and sister as well.

> *Francisco wasn't a bad guy...He'd grown up in Texas and then in a little community in the southwestern part of the state, here. Francisco was just doing the best he could. These were terrible burdens he had on his back, for a 28-year-old guy. He also had his little sister living with him. She was still in high school. I'm not sure where the parents were, but he was raising his little sister. He had a little brother living with him and his brother was in high school. He had a little family situation set up there and he was trying to make ends meet. I've seen people that have worked hard during their lifetimes, like Francisco had.*

Mani separates himself from the supervisors by suggesting that, in their whiteness, they made untrue assumptions about Francisco. Despite his supervisors' wishes, Officer Sano follows his own version of the 'right' ending:

> *The supervisors were adamant that Francisco be arrested. I didn't care for that idea. I think to them, Francisco was seen as a semi-literate Hispanic. These were white supervisors making the decision. Francisco had just gone through a life threatening situation. He had had enough... Ultimately what happened was I didn't file a case on him. The other two went to prison and I didn't file anything else.*

Once again, the link between identity, moral view and authority is highlighted. Mani believes that the right thing to do is to let Francisco go, in part because he understands Francisco. He has seen others who worked hard as he did; he shares an identity with the man, even though they seem to fall on opposite sides of the law. Officer Sano challenges the authority of his supervisors to know the right thing to do, presuming some narrow-mindedness on their part. He even implicitly challenges the authority of the state to know universally what is right for citizens: he chooses not to arrest Francisco for the marijuana, perhaps because he relates to the experience of financial burdens and hard work. Mani plays down the marijuana sales by emphasizing Francisco's financial responsibilities: to his wife, his home, his sister and his brother.

Personal is Political

While state actors may have a greater right to define what is best because of their positions as state actors, there is much more happening in practice.

Agents of the state bring with them their identities, their moral views and their experiences to recognize and select from the available options for disposing of cases. These actors do not comprise one homogeneous group, enforcing the law or state policies from high rank down. Instead, state actors are heterogeneous, in rank and position, certainly, but also in perspective, which is tightly tied to identity, to moral view and to (perceptions of) lived experiences. Thus claims to know may be more potent when made by state actors, but they are not simple manifestations of formal power. Rather, these are moral claims, claims about the way people (ought to) fit together and who people are (or ought to be). They are often driven by experience, and sometimes serve to contest authority, rather than reproduce it. Individual claims are enforced to the extent that the state agent has the structural authority to do so. Sometimes this happens as a function of policy, sometimes policy must be stretched to fit the case, and sometimes knowledge claims contradict policies. Owing in part to the mix of identity, morality and authority, state agents' actions are complex and not always straightforwardly 'for' the state's interest of self-preservation.

Moreover, the morality claims in these stories were always told to us after the fact of actions that were taken. Moral commitments were deployed to justify whatever actions had been taken and were offered as evidence of who the storyteller is, as in the story told above by Judy, who claims she is a deaf woman and therefore knows the right thing for her client – indeed, knows better than his own, hearing mother does. In the context of the stories presented here, moral justifications were deployed as a story-telling technique to persuade us, as the audience, that the storyteller was a particular kind of good person who used authority to do the right thing.

We strongly suspect that story telling among state agents themselves is deployed, in part, for the same reason. Indeed, in the long hours we spent with them in the field, the workers presented themselves to one another in particularized ways, but often with the intent of establishing their moralities and identities. Moreover, in the context of relating to one another, street-level workers were also fabricating their cultures of work and professions so as to enable a degree of workgroup cohesion amidst depictions of their heterogeneity.

Notes

1   There is another layer, here, another set of subjectivities at play in the making of this story. As a privileged white woman of childbearing age, one author's similarity to the wife positioned her as judge–legitimator of the officer's actions, evidenced by the moral outrage with which he told the story. He assumed that Trish needed no convincing that this was poor mothering and that she should only have to hear what he'd seen to support him and legitimate his choice of actions.

2   SSI stands for Social Security Income.
3   Oralism refers to the use of spoken language both as spoken by the deaf and hearing-impaired and as the lip reading which accompanies that use of language. This form of communication is convenient for hearing people interacting with the deaf and hearing-impaired, but often individuals with hearing disabilities are not able to become oral successfully. In too many cases, children with hearing disabilities are told to focus on oralism and, when unable to master this communication, are left without the ability to communicate at all.
4   The reader may be thinking that the counselor was being tough on a man who was genuinely being discriminated against. The reader may be right. However, analyzing her interviews and stories and spending time with her, we see consciousness raising, especially around disability rights, as one of her top priorities.

6   Cultures of Work:
Incorporating Difference as
Loosely Shared Meanings

Dennis Mumby suggests that 'organization members, as social *actors*, actively participate in the construction of organizational reality through organizational discourse' (1987:113). The most interesting facet of organizational reality, what we call the cultures of work, of the police officers and VR counselors we studied centered on the way difference was incorporated into each organization's set of loosely shared meanings. Specifically, we focus on the way each group of workers incorporates difference: in imagining themselves as part of their bureaucratic environments, doing justice for citizens and depicting a shared meaning of discretionary politics.

Of course, the following analysis of the discourses of difference does not seek to imply that organizational members were uniform in their understandings or their actions. Mary Boyce explains that 'meaning exists that is not shared by all the members within a group ... The shared meaning may appear as the intersection and/or overlap of several different perspectives [or identities] co-existing within a group or as a dominant shared sense of meaning' (1995:107).

Differences in the Perceptions of Bureaucratic Control

One of our early working premises in this study was that vocational rehabilitation counselors and police officers operate under differing amounts of bureaucratic control and that this would contribute to the ways they imagine, act on and even recognize discretionary moments. Our analysis finds that both occupational groups were under a good deal of (always incomplete) bureaucratic control and that the control exercised by members of each group was qualitatively, rather than quantitatively, different. Both counselors and police officers seemed to operate under substantial constraint, but these constraints often may be perceived differently by officers, as compared to counselors.

At Glenville RSA, weekly staff meetings routinely included significant attention to administrative policy revisions sent from higher administrative offices. New policies seemed never to be in full working condition and, in nearly every case we saw, a major policy revision would be followed by smaller weekly changes meant to fine-tune the major revision. For example, in fieldnotes from one staff meeting, one of us wrote:

> a new fee schedule book was distributed, but it had some wrong prices, so they were not to throw out the old schedule, but should throw out the new schedule, and then should wait for the new, new schedule to arrive. The book was about 250 pages long and the problem involved the first twenty pages.

These smaller changes would often be contradictory: one week the change would be to add 'step x' and three weeks later, the change would be to take 'step x' away again. Each week in the staff meetings, a portion of the time was spent negotiating the constant stream of new and changed administrative mandates. One week, a new program introducing 'one-time' expense vouchers[1] created some confusion. Fieldnotes reflect how the collective office interpretation of the program was negotiated through the ambiguity of the written policy:

> Jane asked counselors to imagine when they might use the vouchers. Benita asked about a problem with the rules. No voucher can be written to the family of the client, yet childcare, a likely voucher case, could easily be done by family. Jane said that it would be fine to allow family members to babysit through a one-time voucher. Vouchers are being used because vendors were wanting to use credit cards, which VR can't do. 'One time' distribution of money can be treated creatively, as a one-time check/voucher for an entire semester's worth of childcare. Jane expects questions about these vouchers.

This office's interpretation of that policy is likely to be different from other offices' interpretations of the same policy.[2] The top-down bureaucratic controls were explicitly negotiated as the office adopted the program for its own, in the *ways* that it made the system its own. Moreover, in addition to negotiating *what* the adopted practice will be, there is also a negotiation of *how* adopted practices will be defined in the office. Not only is Jane, the office manager, willing to bend the rule about writing vouchers to family members in the case of childcare, but also she is willing to count a repeated service (babysitting) as a one-time payment (that is, 'childcare for one semester').

The flexibility to maneuver within a ceaseless onslaught of bureaucratic efforts to control was explicitly recognized, assumed and accepted by RSA staff, from supervisor to secretary. Staff struggled with new directives until everyone in the office had a common working knowledge of how 'we,' as a workgroup, would treat this policy. As long as the office as a whole came to an agreement about the way any particular policy should be understood, further deliberation was not necessary. In short, procedures were discussed until a group consensus was achieved (often by top-down tutoring by Jane, the supervisor) and then counselors used the policy with that agreed-upon understanding. The decision-making unit, therefore, was understood to be the office or the workgroup, rather than individual counselors. Once office-wide consistency was achieved, there was little discussion or debate about that particular policy.

However, such a working office consensus was not always achieved quickly. Sometimes directives were taken in and understood a particular way easily, but, at other times, Jane encouraged or even insisted on a dialogue with higher administrators regarding certain problems with their mandates. For example, one required form measured pay periods in inappropriate amounts, such as 'months' instead of 'hours.' This caused a problem for counselors who had to submit complete forms, but struggled to make sense of the conversion and questioned the logic behind the forms. Jane encouraged her counselors to write letters and tell the policy makers at the district level (referred to as 'higher-ups' most of the time) that there were problems with the new forms they had created. Several counselors did this, and Jane collected their letters and added a letter of her own. About a month later, the new policy changes for the day included a revision of that form, as per office feedback.

Jane sought homogeneity within her office, and spent time working to achieve a common understanding among all office workers. Indeed, this seems to be have been a primary intention behind the weekly staff meetings. Everyone acknowledged the possibility that a different office would respond differently to the same policy, but this was not extended to the counselor level. Rather, counselors within the office were expected to handle policies similarly. Ensuring this, all cases were 'staffed' (discussed by the staff) at the weekly meetings. During staffings, the group generally worked together to form a consensus about how a case ought to be handled. It was usually only after all disagreements, if any, had been resolved that Jane gave her formal approval. This brief explanation comes from our fieldnotes.

> Clients are described in terms of age, race, marital status, diagnosis, treatments, progress, current situation, work history, and sometimes referral source. Once the situation is clear to everyone, anyone with any suggestions gives them, a plan is firmed up for the client... and then Jane signs off on it.

Moreover, in one instance, when group consensus could not be achieved, Jane did not approve the case. Fieldnotes from this meeting read:

> Judy presented an IWRP [Individual Written Rehabilitation Plan] in which she
> wanted to send a client (deaf/hard of hearing) to get a Bachelor's degree, but
> another counselor suggested that the client needed only a certificate or at most an
> Associate's. The other counselors and Jane agreed that he may only need a little
> education rather than a lot, much to Judy's dismay. She really seemed to want the
> guy to get through a four-year program, but the other counselors didn't think the
> expense would be justified because his chosen career field could be entered with
> much less education. This case was not signed... Judy was frustrated and was not
> satisfied with the group's lack of support for her plan.

Thus workgroup consensus was a goal expected by Jane and accepted by
counselors. Discretion was to be exercised in the context of group thinking,
which was a centerpiece of the weekly staff meetings.

Things were markedly different at the Glenville PD, most of the time. The
police workgroups that participated in our study presumed the individual
officer to be in control of discretionary moments. While policies were
important to learn and know well, supervisors and officers expressed a
defensive need to empower individual decision making. For example, the
supervisor of the workgroups we studied, Karen Marker, defines 'fairness' in
terms of balancing actual individuals and abstract rules:

> ...that you can deal with people [as] individuals and we should, within this
> framework of what the rules and policies and procedures are, but it's a framework.
> It's not just specific lines on a page. I kind of feel like everybody's got to
> stop...everybody's got a story and I can't just keep applying the rules and regs to
> each of them disregarding what that story is because they vary by large
> increments...We do it every day in disciplinary matters. It's important to weigh
> out what this person did in this set of circumstances.

Similarly, a supervisor of one of the units, Rick Gartner, suggests the need for
individual liberties with respect to resolving cases. He said that an essential
part of justice is 'using discretion, using your own core value base to sometimes make decisions that, at the present time, you think are best... I think it
has to come on kind of an individual case, yet still remain in some parameters
of justice and fairness for people.'

The officers had daily meetings with other officers working the same shift
and often those meetings included a segment on training and homogeneity of
case resolution, but, inevitably, the police officers stressed a need to retain
individual authority to make contextualized decisions. During briefings,
specific situations were sometimes presented and officers would suggest
what to do. Although there was often a variety of suggestions, one possibility
was usually defined as the best by the supervising sergeant, and officers were
instructed accordingly. In fieldnotes, one of us outlined one such moment of
group training:

Training issue: An officer was out on a 911 hangup call. Neighbors report a history of domestic violence at the address. First officer on scene sees the blinds move, indicating that someone is home, although 911 has been trying to get them on the phone since the hangup. There is no blood, no shouting . . . what should you do?

[Right Answer:]
– keep trying the phone
– no records on the guy, whose name was obtained using the license plates on his car
– the apartment manager has no key for the place

[ACTUAL SCENARIO]: using teamwork and a stroke of luck (in the form of an unlocked window), plus a shotgun, police were able to safely enter and scan each room of the house. It was eventually discovered that a cat moved the blinds. [No one was home.]

Although there was a broad discussion about the proper technique of entering this house, Sergeant Ledman upheld one particular, two-person team method of entry. He told the officers that such a strategy of one covering the other and vice versa was how the department intended such situations to be handled. The rhetoric of individual judgment was momentarily abandoned as standard procedure was defined.

However, in practice, individualized judgments – varied, contextualized resolutions to everyday dilemmas – were the most noticeable expression of street and office policy for these police workgroups. Certainly, there were guidelines, but even as such guidelines were identified, a need for contextual cues was included. For example, one sergeant, Rick Gartner, advocated 'an equal application of the law without . . . favor or any preconceived or current prejudices.' However, he was quick to explain that the rule should not be without exceptions, but instead should be understood through

a basic, what I'll call kind of a common ground . . . right and wrongs that I think, we, as human beings, can all agree on. And an example would be a mother who is honestly stealing food for her starving baby or something to that effect. Certainly by the letter of the law, that would be defined as a theft.

His own explanation of this common ground focuses on the *exceptions* rather than the rule he was attempting to define. Implicitly, Rick is talking about laws against stealing and the police policy to arrest thieves. Explicitly, he is honed in on the exceptions, when *not* to arrest, as the unlikely event in which a person has been defined as 'honestly stealing.'[3]
Even in situations where the supervisors felt clear about policies and felt that exceptions were unlikely, individual judgment and exceptionalism entered into the resolution. This is revealed at the end of an interview exchange between the supervising Lieutenant, Karen Marker, and one of us:

Interviewer: So it's like paying attention to the context of people's circumstances that is kind of your application of fairness. Looking at what's going on in that particular case and then weighing that against both the formal rule and the spirit of that rule.

Lieutenant: And what discretion am I allowed in this set of circumstances. I mean, if it's a hard, fast rule that I don't have any discretion on, for heaven's sake. If you smoke marijuana when you're a police officer, we're done talking about this. There is no question. You're out of here.

Yet, in the story about the fireman's suicide described in Chapter 5, a different supervisor, who realized that the deceased fireman may have been using cocaine and may have even had a problem with the drug,[4] used his decision-making authority[5] to conceal evidence of the drug. Thus, even when policy is abstractly presumed to be inviolable, the actual practice is to use individual judgment and to enforce the privilege of personal authority at least as strongly as law and policy are enforced. Thus, where the RSA staff assumed that discretion was available to offices and were concerned with unifying decision making to achieve *office-wide* cohesion, the police officers, conversely, assumed that an external cohesion (a fraternity, or illusion thereof) was understood and therefore focused on protecting *individual* discretion. We believe these two differing trends regarding bureaucratic control and discretionary decision making also factored into contrasting ideas about the way client differences should (and could) be handled.

Justice, Discretion and the Handling of Client Differences

The RSA office serves distinct groups of clients, and each group has special needs. For example, hearing-impaired clients need interpreters, who can be extremely expensive, but who are integral to a client's rehabilitation. Severely mentally ill clients might need extended counseling and job supports, keeping these cases open for longer periods of time and therefore requiring more attention from the counselor than other clients might expect. The disparate treatment given to different kinds of clients never seemed to arouse a sense of injustice in our observations. Instead, counselors seemed quite confident in their belief that, although some got more money and others got more time, to the extent possible, each client got fair treatment by the counselor and by the agency as a whole. Jane explained,

[The deaf] need interpreters the whole way through. That, that adds on a lot more cost. So when you look at costs of caseloads, you're gonna see the blind and you're gonna see the deaf, really high cost. You'll see spinal cord injuries sometimes high cost, particularly van modifications, if we're doing those. Or a wheelchair, getting a wheelchair. So special treatment, no. More stuff, yeah.

One counselor explains that the ultimate concern is not how much money (or 'stuff') a client receives, but rather that the client gets what he or she individually needs. Difference is a simple part of the equation, but instead of looking at the difference in *services received*, Sharon emphasized the difference in *services needed*:

> Everyone is wanting something different or with different abilities so that, you know, I don't offer people different things because of who they are. It's just maybe their abilities and their wants. You know, I mean the welder lady doesn't want to go to dog school[6] ... That's why it's about fairness ... and looking at it so that I look at each case the same way ... it's what fits the person and what they need ... So they're not being gypped because this guy got $7000. You know, maybe he needed some extra work or extended support... The end result is the same.

Most of the counselors were able to see the differences among their clients this way, both within one caseload type and compared across types. Rehabilitation plans were written for individuals, not as office policy, but as one-on-one contracts between the counselor and the client. Counselors were clearly aware (and often reminded us) that what was great for one client may be inappropriate for another. Client difference was not only tolerated, but anticipated. Moreover, counselors were acutely aware of differences between kinds of caseloads and readily acknowledged that budgets were justly uneven.[7] Despite this comfort and acceptance of client differences, and the corresponding differences in what clients were able to get from the agency, when asked to define 'justice' in the abstract, the counselors quite often pointed to a sameness or equality model. Counselors described justice using words like 'equal treatment' (Thomas), or 'equal amounts and equal treatment' (Betty). One counselor said, 'I think of justice as being fair, in balance, more equality ... making sure that everybody comes with, you know, the same privileges, er, you know, they're offered the same kinds of things' (Sharon). Thus, for the RSA staff, the abstract notions of justice often were equity-based, and the practical enactment of justice assumed difference.

Perhaps this contradiction is part of why so many participants said that being asked to define justice was a difficult task. From the office supervisor, Jane ('That's a hard question'), to a new counselor, Betty ('Why are you asking me such hard questions?'), most participants openly struggled with the question, 'What is justice?' An implicit recognition that both sameness and difference are involved in justice lies within the seeming contradiction of abstract and practical responses. In the RSA, staff clearly wanted to use their attention to difference to achieve what they thought was best for clients. Difference talk tended to be couched in comments about what was 'needed' by the client and what the client was 'able' to do or achieve. The talk about 'fairness' tended to assume the question, 'What is fair for the client?'[8] Even client grievances evoked no fear from the counselors, as long as they believed they had acted to do what was just (or right or fair) for an individual client, almost regardless of policy.

The police also explicitly addressed the matter of difference, but they often did so to loosen the rules, to give themselves more flexibility within the regulations. Lieutenant Marker says she 'can't just keep applying rules and regs to each of them disregarding what that story is.' She wants to protect her right to be right about cases. In the interview Karen expressed her hope that she has 'a decent evaluation of what the right thing is' and advocated a grounds from which to know. 'It's got to be experience and knowledge and attitude and discretion and all of those things are just little pieces of me. This is just me. This is how I would answer...' Thus she advocates that individual experience be the authority to know how the rules ought to be enforced.

Wendy Burton, a sergeant, when asked about discretion, jumped to the potential for its misuse, and began an impromptu defense of what had never been attacked.

> I'll get back to kind of the fact that police departments are made up of people and we hire people from all walks of life. And sometimes we get people who appear fair and just when we hire them. Maybe they slip through the system or [it] may be their front or maybe their reality and, on the other hand, we probably hire people that are as good faith and just and fair as that can be and something about the job or the system has a tendency to taint them and they will go about doing things that maybe aren't proper. And those things are very, very hard to defend against.

Accepting the inherent potential for discrimination or other misbehavior validates the discretionary system. Officer Ray Carillo describes the intensity under which discretionary decisions might be made: 'this is a unique kind of job, where in one second I might be just sitting here talking with you and in thirty seconds I might be chasing down some... suspect and you have tenths of a second to make a decision... shoot, not shoot.' Although we didn't see this kind of action during our fieldwork, still this officer used that extreme scenario to demonstrate the importance of supervisors defending officers' decisions, arguing that there is no time to think of repercussions in the heat of the moment. Thus, for the officers, in contrast to the counselors, discretion was often defined in terms of what was most fair to the *officer doing the job*, rather than the client (that is, victim or suspect). There were exceptions, such as the one cited above, where Sergeant Gartner defended discretion for fear of cases of 'honest stealing,' although none of the thefts that were investigated during the period of observation were considered for their 'honesty.' Given that no officer questioned the moral integrity of the presumed criminal, one cannot help but wonder if this verbal example of 'honest stealing' is merely a way to make palatable the notion that individual officers need to have latitude in the way particular cases are treated.

Different Conceptions of Discretion

Thus we found some occupational difference between the counselors and the police officers in how they maintained their autonomy while forging a shared understanding of discretionary politics. Where RSA counselors were likely to advocate some power to bend and shape the rules in order to do what the *counselor believed* was best for the client, the police were likely to defend their *freedom* to bend and shape the rules in order to facilitate how they do their jobs. In practice, counselors seemed quite content to plan the acceptable range of bending and shaping of the rules as a group: the supervisor and the counselors negotiated the domain of flexibility *as an office workgroup*. They recognized the likelihood of other offices having different freedoms and limitations, but sought to agree among themselves about how certain policies would be understood within their workgroup. In this sense, an office-specific culture emerged, as counselors sought intra-office homogeneity with very little concern for the way other offices treated policy.

The opposite seems true of the police officers. They defended the *abstract* freedom to use discretion, without specific regard for where an officer worked. Despite the range of different moral determinations about the 'right' thing to do, particularly as evidenced around notions of family, officers insisted that all officers should have a right to use their own judgment in particular cases. As part of the job, officers explicitly desired a department-backed right to be right. In contrast to the VR counselors who sought office or working group homogeneity, the officers sought to protect the heterogeneity of resolution strategies and rule enforcements both within their department and more generally across an imagined 'fraternity.'

Notes

1 Typically, services are rendered and then billed to the client, who, in turn, submits the bill to RSA for payment. Sometimes, services are rendered by vendors, who take requisitions from clients, render services, but charge RSA directly. At other times, services cannot be rendered because the client cannot pay 'up front' and the service provider will not wait for the bill to be submitted to RSA. It is for these instances in particular that the vouchers were intended.

2   For example, another office might be more firm about the mandate to not use the vouchers to pay family members.

3   Although Sergeant Gartner selects an example which appeals to context and humanity, the kind of discretion we saw involved more unusual kinds of moralized, identified judgments. Recall that one cop identified Francisco's pot sales as 'trying to take care of family,' where another cop identified the same man as a criminal who should be arrested.

4   Given that the man's death was by suicide and that he was agitated and stressed about money before his death, one cannot rule out that possibility.

5   The officer may have merely allowed someone else to use his or her discretion that way, as the story is told in the third person.

6   These are two of her cases, one a woman wanting to become trained as a welder and the other a woman wanting to become a dog trainer. She is reminding us that the cases are individual and that what is ideal for one client is undesired by another.

7   However, the lack of money squabbles may have been due to a healthy supply of funds. Even as one counselor's budget came up short, another had money to spare. Fieldnotes from one staff meeting read: 'Each counselor is supposed to basically balance her/his quarterly budget (ends in Sept.) and be sure that no additional funds are needed. I was astonished that this was not a tense matter. Instead of the tight, panicky voice one might expect when someone is talking about needing twice as many funds as s/he has, one counselor (who needed to literally double his funds from $5000 to $10 000) responded without any emotion in his voice whatsoever, as if borrowing a book. Another counselor said she had plenty. It was hardly the scrimp-and-save discussion that I had anticipated' (8/18/97). There is no certain reason to expect fighting over plentiful resources even if they are distributed unevenly.

8   Or, much less frequently, 'What is fair to the taxpayers?'

7 Conclusions: Reimagining Discretion as Exceptionalism

The state's goods and services are administered – law is realized – only as a mixture of abstraction and context. Faceless law interacts with the many faces of its agents and clients. It may be shaped in, understood through or undermined by the active identities of its individual representatives, as well as their creative knowledge of others' identities. These representatives share identities as state agents and, more specifically, as particular kinds of state agents. Groups of state agents share what we have called an organizational culture, parts of which are shared with other similar state actors, as a fraternity of police extending beyond one's department, and parts of which are unique to a particular office.

Identity and morality are mutually constitutive and mutually legitimated. Identities are often created through moral action, even as one's acceptable range of possible actions is circumscribed through identity. Those acting under the identity of state actors, either police or VR staff, act with the unique power and authority to enact laws: momentarily to make concrete what is otherwise always and only abstract, uninterpreted. By bringing law to life, state agents bring life to law. Power is laced with identity; state authorities' actions are often moral actions. Identified interpretations of the 'right outcome,' the 'moral action' or 'justice' often drive and legitimate the decisions made by state actors. Thus, endorsed by the state's authority, police officers, VR counselors, and other state agents have more right to be right than other citizens generally have. The power to name and define situations and their just outcomes lies disproportionately with state actors, relative to most other kinds of citizens.

Morality and power intersect in the daily decisions of police officers and VR counselors. The ultimate responsibility for the distribution of the country's goods and services, including protection, liberty or punishment, lies with the street-level bureaucrats who lend ears to tone-deaf policies and who lend eyes to color-blind laws. Any notion of impartiality is dispelled and neutrality can only be recognized as a mythic ideal. Certainly, state agents do not act with

95

total liberty, unguided by policy and law. However, how laws are interpreted and realized is an undeniably partial practice, as we discussed in Chapter 5. Beyond policy and legal limitations, the assuming of an identity as state agent involves some subjectification, and a shared common sense about the 'right outcome' emerges and partly defines how state agents do their jobs.

Of course this common sense does not translate to full homogeneity among state agents. We have shown in this case how identity, moral view and organizational culture interrupt the abstraction of law and influence the ways that laws are enacted, policies enforced, situations defined and outcomes evaluated. At its core, this interruption reveals how state agents subjectify citizens in particular, value-laden ways, enforcing such subjectifications through their decisions about how and whether to distribute the state's protections, liberties and coercions. As opposed to a notion that state actors are primarily rule-bound, this study has revealed that rules can be used to justify an array of different ends and that state actors rely on tropes other than the rules (like identity and moral orientation) to know how to act.

Thus human agency in dispensing law is a given. Efforts to reduce or eliminate workers' discretion must concede that, no matter how narrowly a rule is written, it still leaves space for the worker to interject him or herself into the actual human transaction of law or policy. Our findings reinforce the point that discretion is an unavoidable facet of bureaucracy.

We have contrasted our view of the relationship between identity and morality to earlier views which assert that there is a gender component to morality: simply, that gender identity influences moral orientation. Although earlier work articulated two gender-linked moral orientations, an ethic of justice and an ethic of care, ambiguous research results about the significance of that link prompted us to question the usefulness of a problematically binary understanding. Indeed, we have shown throughout this text that identity is richly layered and certainly more complex than the gender binary can reveal. Moreover, we have shown that non-hypothetical moral decisions indeed seem to be influenced and/or justified according to identity, but that this occurs in a manner which is much more convoluted than a simple binary orientation model. Given that we find identity to be so much more complexly layered than a two-tiered approach can serve, we must raise the question of whether it is a worthy cause to continue studying morality or moral orientations in abstract ways.

Another path of exploration was taken by Suzanne Leland and Steven Maynard-Moody, collaborators in this research endeavor, in another of the project's sites. They argue that state agents are driven by a sense of accountability, but they may be operating with competing understandings of the principal to whom they are accountable (see Leland and Maynard-Moody, 1998). They may, for example, define themselves as principally accountable to the agency and therefore may emphasize the rules and regulations in their most narrow sense. Similarly, state agents may define their principal accountability as being towards each other. In that case, all possible actions would be evaluated first in terms of their consequence for others holding the same or similar jobs. Alternatively, they may prioritize the taxpayer as the entity to whom they feel accountable and decisions are then made according to prudent fiscal priorities. Still another way to define state agents' accountability is as being directly to the client, and the corresponding drive would be to use as many resources as are available to assist the client in reaching her or his goal. In any case, it could reasonably be argued that each of these orientations was available in the stories told by the workers.

While we insist that identity and morality are inseparable from the law that is realized on the street and in the offices of state agents, we wonder how these identities and moralities look in an analysis that is not a microanalysis. In other words, how do these identities and moralities which underpin state agents' knowledge of how to administer the state start to cumulate as the agents' actions are taken as a group instead of as individual stories? What happens to our analysis as the hypothetical and the non-hypothetical are taken together and as the data are examined at the group level? These questions may direct further analysis and inform another discussion about identity and power and the moralizing subjectification of political subjects.

Clearly, given our understanding of identity, we do not suppose that discretion can be controlled, reduced or otherwise taken away from those who work as state actors in contact with citizens. Not only is this unrealistic, but it also denies that the individuals who make decisions on behalf of the state on a routine basis can have expertise that should be brought to bear on those decisions. In short, not only could we not eliminate discretion among state agents, we are not certain that we want to anyway. Instead, what we suggest is a reimagining of the so-called 'problem' of discretion. Perhaps, in fact, discretion is not really the problem at all.

Indeed, the state agents who participated in this study generally believed that they made good decisions about the 'right' thing to do. As they endeavored to enact justice and to do the 'right' thing, they used their decision-making authority to evoke their own visions of the best outcomes for the situations that presented themselves. The problem seems to be revealed, however, when different workers have different visions of the 'right' ending to any given story, as evidenced in Francisco's story, in which one officer, sharing a racial and class identity with the suspect, wants to identify that suspect as a victim, while his superiors who do not share the identity match want to arrest the suspect. In this case, the problem is not discretion, as both decision makers can choose, but rather exceptionalism, as one officer chooses to a cut a break and another officer does not.

Efforts to reduce discretion seem to be seeking to reduce exceptionalism, both for the better and for the worse, in hopes of a system that is impartial and undiscriminating, however impossible the goal may seem. What we have found is that the identities and the closely related moral views of the workers themselves had something to do with that exceptionalism. At times officers 'cut breaks' for those to whom they related, such as Francisco the marijuana dealer, and sometimes reacted firmly to those with whom they did not, such as Angela, the drunk and pregnant street woman. If we are correct that *exceptionalism* is the problem, then we think our research raises questions that are important for policy makers and key staff at state agencies. We argue that discretion is an uncontrollable given, and that it is riddled with the beliefs and orientations of those who have enough power to own discretion.

The question at hand, though, is whether the inability to remove discretion from state workers' hands necessarily means that we are unable to reduce or otherwise alter the current patterns of exceptionalism. What links can we find between the identities of workers and the kinds of exceptions that are made? If our analysis applies to other agencies beyond the two we studied intensely, we would want to know whether diversifying workforces with regard to identities might also diversify the recipients of exceptions. Could we create work cultures through worker training or diversity that would pass along exceptions to citizens in a new pattern? Could this, in turn, have the effect of legitimating the law in new ways for an ever-increasing diversity of citizen subjects?

Our analysis shows that exceptionalism is related to the interplay of identities and moralities of state workers in the streets and in the halls. Although they may not be related in any readily predictable binary way, still moral views, identities and work cultures clearly move with the sway of chaotic human interaction. Although organizations such as the ones we studied can not buffer themselves against that chaos, they can alter the constellations of identities and the corresponding moral orientations that represent the front-line decision-making authority. Such organizations could alter whom they endow with the right to be right in ways that have an impact on the way goods and services are delivered at the line level.

Appendix A: Initial Interview

Thank you for participating in this project. Do you have any questions about your participation or the grant before we start? (Remember you may stop the recorder any time to ask questions.)

1 What is your job title? How long have you been doing this? How long have you been working at this agency? Have you had other related jobs? Please describe. What made you become a rehabilitation counselor?

2 Work relations: What is it like to work here?

- Probe feelings about the work? (e.g. scary, overwhelming, boring, satisfying, etc.)

- Probe feelings about relations with other workers (e.g. cooperative, contentious, friendly, cold, etc.)

- Probe feelings about relations with supervisors (e.g. cooperative, bossy, appreciated, unappreciated, etc.)

3 Most offices are made up of people from different social groups – genders, ethnicities, classes, able-bodiedness, etc. How do these distinctions relate to how counselors get along in your agency? How do they relate to hiring practices in your office? Would you say that these groups are fairly represented in your office?

4 Client relations:

- Can you describe the typical client(s)?

- How are clients similar to you? How do they differ from you?

- Who are the easiest clients to serve? Who are the hardest?

- Are there any complaints from particular groups of clients?

5 Identify critical incidents. Looking back over your time with GRSA, can you think of any incidents that changed the way you do your work? These

events could be anything: a particular case that changed policy, a shift in funding or leadership, or any event that resulted in a change in the way routine work is done. When did the event occur and how (or why) did it impact the way you do things?

6   We are all members of different social groups or affiliations. Some of these pertain to your sex, race, ethnicity, able-bodiedness or social class. We are also members of occupational groups. Which of these group memberships are most important to your sense of self? (Feel free to add new groups to the list.)

7   Is there anything you want to add for the tape?

Appendix B: Exit Interview

Research Project:
Discretion and Public Service Delivery
Funded by the National Science Foundation

Principle Investigator: Michael Musheno
Research Associates: Duane Hall and Trish Oberweis
School of Justice Studies
Arizona State University
Tempe AZ 85287-0403
(602)965-7698
fax: (602)965-9199
e-mail: Musheno@ASU.EDU

Pseudonym _____

Please circle the letter of the single best response to each of the following questions.

1   How heavy was your workload in the past month?
    a   Light
    b   A bit light
    c   Just about right
    d   Heavy
    e   Too heavy to keep up with

2   How much authority do you have in determining what tasks to perform day-to-day?
    a   None
    b   Little
    c   Some
    d   Quite a bit
    e   Very much

3   To what extent does your agency have clear-cut, reasonable goals and objectives?
    a   To a very small extent
    b   To a little extent
    c   To some extent
    d   To a great extent
    e   To a very great extent

4   To what extent did you follow standard operating procedures or practices to do your major tasks in the last month?
    a   To no extent
    b   Little extent
    c   Some extent
    d   Great extent
    e   Very great extent

5   How much authority do you have in establishing rules and procedures about how your work is to be done?
    a   None
    b   Little
    c   Some
    d   Quite a bit
    e   Very much

6   When considering the various situations that arise in performing your work, what percentage of the time do you have written procedures for dealing with them?

   a   0–20%
   b   21–40%
   c   41–60%
   d   61–80%
   e   81–100%

7   How precisely do these written rules and procedures specify how your major tasks are to be done?

   a   Very general
   b   Mostly general
   c   Somewhat specific
   d   Quite specific
   e   Very specific

8   How much authority do you have in handling problems that do not fit standard operating procedures?

   a   None
   b   Little
   c   Some
   d   Quite a bit
   e   Very much

9   What percentage of the time are you generally sure of what the outcomes of your work efforts will be?

   a   40% or less
   b   41–60%
   c   61–75%
   d   76–90%
   e   91% or more

10 When it comes to working with clients, how different are the day-to-day situations?

   a   Completely different
   b   Very different
   c   Quite a bit different
   d   Mostly the same
   e   Very much the same

11   All in all, how satisfied are you with your job?

    a   Unsatisfied
    b   Somewhat unsatisfied
    c   Satisfied
    d   Quite a bit satisfied
    e   Very satisfied

12   How easy is it for you to know whether you did your work correctly?

    a   Very difficult
    b   Quite difficult
    c   Somewhat easy
    d   Quite easy
    e   Very easy

13   I believe that the manager in my organization is paid fairly.

    a   Strongly agree
    b   Somewhat agree
    c   Somewhat disagree
    d   Strongly disagree

14   To what extent do you perform the same tasks from day to day?

    a   To a very little extent
    b   To a little extent
    c   To some extent
    d   To a great extent
    e   To a very great extent

15   To what extent are the resources you have to work with adequate?

    a   To a very small extent
    b   To a little extent
    c   To some extent
    d   To a great extent
    e   To a very great extent

16   How much feeling of loyalty do you have toward this agency?

    a   None
    b   Very little
    c   Some
    d   Quite a bit
    e   Very strong

17 I am more concerned about fair compensation than about fair treatment at work.

    a Strongly agree
    b Somewhat agree
    c Somewhat disagree
    d Strongly disagree

18 I feel the compensation I receive for my work is fair.

    a Strongly agree
    b Somewhat agree
    c Somewhat disagree
    d Strongly disagree

19 In performing your major task, how different are the day-to-day situations?

    a Completely different
    b Very different
    c Quite a bit different
    d Mostly the same
    e Very much the same

20 How much of your work deals directly with clients face-to-face?

    a None
    b About 25%
    c About 50%
    d About 75%
    e All of my work

21 I am concerned about the differences in pay between the front-line staff and the manager in my organization.

    a Strongly agree
    b Somewhat agree
    c Somewhat disagree
    d Strongly disagree

22 I am concerned about the differences in pay between front-line staff and managers in society in general.

    a Strongly agree
    b Somewhat agree
    c Somewhat disagree
    d Strongly disagree

23 Which of the following should be taken into account in deciding how to distribute scholarship money to applicants to professional graduate programs?

    a Scholarships should be given to applicants according to how much they need the money in order to attend graduate school.

    b Scholarship money should be given to applicants according to how hard they have tried to get prepared for graduate school.

    c Scholarship money should be given to applicants based on their grades and general admission test scores.

    d Scholarship money should be given to applicants in such a way that the smallest scholarships are not much less than the largest awards.

24 The role of government should be to help people.

    a Strongly agree
    b Somewhat agree
    c Somewhat disagree
    d Strongly disagree

25 When government provides welfare benefits such as disability, unemployment compensation, and early retirement pensions it only makes people not want to work.

    a Strongly agree
    b Somewhat agree
    c Somewhat disagree
    d Strongly disagree

26 It is the responsibility of government to meet everyone's needs, even in case of sickness, poverty, unemployment and old age.

    a Strongly agree
    b Somewhat agree
    c Somewhat disagree
    d Strongly disagree

27 If someone has a high social or economic position, that indicates the person has special abilities.

    a Strongly agree
    b Somewhat agree
    c Somewhat disagree
    d Strongly disagree

28 I would like to live in a society where the government does nothing except provide for national defense and police protection so that people could be left alone to earn whatever they could.

    a Strongly agree
    b Somewhat agree
    c Somewhat disagree
    d Strongly disagree

29 Please choose the category that best describes your political views.

    a Extremely liberal
    b Liberal
    c Slightly liberal
    d Moderate, middle of the road
    e Slightly conservative
    f Conservative
    g Extremely conservative

A few questions remain to be addressed interview style:

1 What does the word 'justice' mean to you? Are there groups or types of people who are treated unjustly in America today? (If yes) Who?

2 Do you feel that there are any kinds of people who get special treatment by your agency? Is that fair? Are there others that are discriminated against by your agency?

3 Are there any agency rules or procedures that you feel are unfair?

Appendix C: Sketchbook for Storytellers

Instructions for Story Sketches

Over the next several weeks, we would like you to use this sketchbook to write down a rough outline of 2–3 different stories. These stories should describe situations that take place within your department during this time, or that you might remember from the past. The rough outlines will help you remember the story when you tell it to us verbally later; you will not be required to share these notes with us.

We are interested in stories about how or when your own beliefs about fairness or unfairness helped you make decisions. At times your beliefs may have conflicted with the department's formal and informal policies. At other times, policies may have facilitated your reliance on your own beliefs.

Stories could involve an encounter between you and citizens; they could also be about encounters between you and your department or between you and other members of your department. You may also retell a story that happened to someone else, even if you are not a character in the story.

The stories should, as much as possible:

1 have a plot or storyline with a beginning, middle and end,

2 tell us who the characters are,

3 explain the relationship between the characters,

4 describe the feelings of the characters toward each other and the event(s),

5 include a description of the setting and circumstances in which the event(s) occurred.

You don't need to put all this in your notes; we will ask you about these details when you tell us your stories. Just note enough so that you can recreate the story when we come back to interview you.

We will contact you from time to time to set an appointment to hear and record the stories. After all the stories are collected, we will meet with you to discuss them. The stories you tell will be kept confidential. Names of people and organizations within your stories will be changed to protect the identities of characters involved. We will, however, identify the name of the metropolitan area in our research products.

Thank you for participating. If you have any questions, please contact Professor Michael Musheno at Arizona State University, School of Justice Studies, Box 870403, Tempe AZ 85287; or call 965-7698.

Appendix D: Codebook

Story Codes

Interrupts (INT): a premature halt in the action sequence or a shift from one action sequence to another. An interrupt is often, but not always, associated with change of place and characters.

Repetition (REP): a restatement of a descriptive or action detail with or without variation.

Symbols/signs/artifacts (SYM): objects or words that are presented in the story that connote meaning beyond their narrow meaning. Examples: bullet wound scars, accommodation ribbons, pictures.

Causation (CAU): causal attribution: statement that infers an 'if/then' relationship between actions, motives and so on. For example, a police officer justifies use of deadly force: 'If he wouldn't have come so close to me, I wouldn't have had to shoot;' 'Being on crack gave him super powers.'

Thematic Codes

Decision norms (DN) Reason from the perspective of following the rules or *legality/rules (DN-LAW)*; doing what was equitable, fair, impartial, or *justice (DN-JUS)*; acting to protect the good, acting against the bad, or *morality (DN-MOR)*; looking out for me, or *self-interest (DN-SIN)*; protecting the profession, seeing to the reputation of the organization, or *organizational interest (DN-ORG)*; and doing what the situation calls for, or *pragmatism (DN-PRAG)*.

Decision Rules (DR) Follow the rule *(DR-FOL)*; ignore the rule *(DR-IGN)*; bend the rule *(DR-BND)*; subvert or take action against the rule *(DN-SUB)*.

Instructions: For story and thematic codes, mark with brackets in the right margins the text segments that are coded. Mark any and all codes that apply to that text. First coder uses red; second uses blue. Mark all disagreements by circling the code and flag the text area.

Consequences to Street Level Worker (CON)   What happens to the worker as a result of decision or action. For example, nothing, punished, rewarded.

Worker affect (WA)   Worker depictions of feelings in the context of being a member of a profession, working the streets, interacting with others, including expressions of fear, satisfaction, bitterness.

Worker self-identity (WI)   Who one is, or depicting oneself as an American, a worker, as gendered, as family-oriented, sexualized or racialized, as ethnically embedded, as religiously inclined.

Client worth (CW)   Characterization of the client as deserving, lazy, flawed, caring.

Workplace relational dynamics (WD)   Depicting relations and interactions in the workplace between subject/storyteller/interviewee and *subordinate (WD-SUB)*; *supervisor (WD-SUP)*; *fellow worker (WD-WKR)*; and other *organizations*, such as inter-agency relations *(WD-ORG)*.

Street relational dynamics (SD)   Depicting, at times stereotypically, relations and interactions on the job between subject/storyteller/interviewee and *client (SD-CLT)*; *student (SD-STD)*; *suspect (SD-SUS)*; *victim (SD-VIC)*; *groups* of citizens such as rich, poor or women *(SD-GRP)*; *media (SD-MED)*; *advocacy groups (SD-ADV)*; and *public*, as in protecting the public *(SD-PUB)*.

Organizational culture (OC)   The work atmosphere, as collegial, as conflicted, as divided, as in transition, and the relation of worker to organization.

Place/space (PS)   Depictions of setting where one is doing work, including expression about doing work in public places (for example, street corners) as distinct from private places (such as a citizen's home).

Resources (RES)   The characterizations of resources available to do the job, including time, how workers cope with deficiencies in resources and engage in rationing.

Critical Events (CE)   Changes in key personnel, in organizational process; dramatic news about the organization or particular workers as reported in the media.

Bibliography

Aaronson, David, C., Thomas Dienes and Michael Musheno (1978), 'Changing the Public Drunkenness Laws: The Impact of Decriminalization', *Law and Society Review*, 3.

Allport, F.H. (1924), *Social Psychology*, Boston: Houghton-Mifflin.

Althusser, Louis (n.d.) 'Ideology and Ideological State Apparatuses (Notes Toward an Investigation)', reprinted in Ben Brewster (trans.) (1991), *Lenin and Philosophy, and Other Essays*, London: New Left Books.

Aronowitz, Stanley (1995), 'Reflections on Identity', in John Rajchman (ed.), *The Identity in Question*, New York: Routledge.

Bantz, Charles, R. (1993), *Understanding Organizations: Interpreting Organizational Communication Cultures*, Columbia, SC: University of South Carolina.

Bauman, Zygmunt (1993), *Postmodern Ethics*, Oxford: Blackwell Publishers.

Bauman, Zygmunt (1996), 'From Pilgram to Tourist – Or A Short History of Identity', in S. Hall and P. du Gay (eds), *Questions of Cultural Identity*, London: Sage.

Bayley, David and Egon Bittner (1984), 'Learning the Skills of Policing', *Law and Contemporary Problems*, 47.

Benhabib, Seyla (1987), 'The Generalized and the Concrete Other: The Kohlberg–Gilligan Controversy and Moral Theory', in E.F. Kittay and D.T. Meyers (eds), *Women and Moral Theory*, Totowa, NJ: Rowman & Littlefield.

Boyce, Mary E. (1995), 'Collective Centring and Collective Sense-Making in the Stories and Storytelling of One Organization', *Organization Studies*, 16.

Brehm, John and Scott Gates (1997), *Working, Shirking, and Sabotage: a Bureaucratic Response to a Democratic Public*, Ann Arbor: University of Michigan Press.

Brodkin, Evelyn (1997), 'Inside the Welfare Contract: Discretion and Accountability in State Welfare Administration', *Social Service Review*, March.

Butler, Judith (1990), *Gender Trouble: Feminism and the Subversion of Identity*, New York: Routledge.

113

Butler, Judith (1992), 'Contingent Foundations: Feminism and the Question of Postmodernism', in Judith Butler and Joan Scott (eds), *Feminists Theorize the Political*, New York: Routledge.

Butler, Judith (1995), 'Discussion' in John Rajchman (ed.), *The Identity in Question*, New York: Routledge.

Campbell, Donald and H. Laurence Ross (1968), 'The Connecticut Crackdown on Speeding', *Law and Society Review*, 3.

Conley, John M. and William M. O'Barr (1990), *Rules Versus Relationships*, Chicago: University of Chicago Press.

Crank, John (1994), 'Watchman and Community: Myth and Institutionalization in Policing', *Law and Society Review*, 28.

Crank, John (1998), *Understanding Police Culture*, Cincinnati, OH: Anderson Publishing.

Crenshaw, Kimberle (1995), 'Mapping the Margins: Intersectionality, Identity Politics and Violence Against Women of Color', in Dan Danielsen and Karen Engle (eds), *After Identity*, New York: Routledge.

Davis, Kenneth Culp (1971), *Discretionary Justice*, Chicago: University of Chicago Press.

Derrida, Jacques (1978), 'Structure, Sign and Play in Discourse of the Human Sciences', in Jacques Derrida, *Writing and Difference*, trans. Alan Bass, Chicago: University of Chicago Press.

Dobash, R. Emerson and Russell P. Dobash (1992), *Women, Violence and Social Change*, London: Routledge.

Engel, David M. and Frank W. Munger (1996), 'Rights, Remembrance and the Reconciliation of Difference', *Law and Society Review*, 30 (1).

Ewick, Patricia and Susan Silbey (1995), 'Subversive Stories and Hegemonic Tales: Toward a Sociology of Narrative', *Law and Society Review*, 29 (2).

Ewick, Patricia and Susan Silbey (1998), *The Common Place of Law: Stories from Everyday Life*, Chicago: University of Chicago Press.

Foucault, Michel (1980), *Power/Knowledge*, ed. Colin Gordon, New York: Pantheon Books.

Foucault, Michel (1988), 'The Political Technology of Individuals', in Luther H. Martin, Huck Gutman and Patrick H. Hutton (eds), *Technologies of the Self*, Amherst: University of Massachusetts Press.

Freidman, Marilyn (1987), 'Care and Context in Moral Reasoning', in E.F. Kittay and D.J. Meyers (eds), *Women and Moral Theory*, Totawa, NJ: Rowman & Littlefield.

Galanter, Marc (1975), 'Why the Haves Come Out Ahead: Speculations on the Limits of Legal Change', *Law and Society Review*, 9.

Gallup, Jane (1983), '*Quand nos lèvres s'écrivent*: Irigary's Body Politic', *Romantic Review*, 74 (1).

Gamson, William (1992), *Talking Politics*, New York: Cambridge University Press.

Garfinkel, Harold (1967), *Studies in Ethnomethodology*, Englewood Cliffs, NJ: Prentice-Hall.

Garvey, Gerald (1993), *Facing the Bureaucracy: Living and Dying in a Public Agency*, San Francisco: Jossey-Bass Publishers.

Gilligan, Carol (1982), *In a Different Voice*, Cambridge, MA: Harvard University Press.

Gilligan, Carol (1986), 'Reply by Carol Gilligan', *Signs*, 11 (2).

Glass, Gene, George Tiao and Thomas Maguire (1971), 'The 1960 Revision of German Divorce Laws: Analysis of Data as a Time-Series Quasi-Experiment', *Law and Society Review*, 5.

Glenville, City of (1995), *1995 Statistical Report*, municipal document.

Glenville, City of (1996), *1996 Statistical Report*, municipal document.

Glenville, City of (1997), *1997 Statistical Report*, municipal document.

Glenville Police Department (n.d.), 'Community Policing Philosophy', internal pamphlet.

Glenville Police Department (n.d.), 'Moving Towards Community Policing: Strategies for Transition', organizational text.

Glenville Police Department (1991), 'An Initial Assessment of Business and Residential Members in the Beat P Community', internal document, May.

Glenville Police Department (1992), 'A Follow-Up Assessment of Business and Residential Members in the Beat P Community', internal document, June.

Glenville Police Department (1992), 'Community Policing: An Initial Assessment of the Residential Members in Beat L', internal document, Summer.

Glenville Police Department (1993), 'Innovative Neighborhood Oriented Policing Program: Implementation Guide', organizational text.

Glenville Police Department (1996), 'Application 1996 National League of Cities *Excellence in Community Policing* Awards Competition', internal document.

Glenville Police Department, Community Services Department (n.d.), 'Youth Citizen Police Academy', information booklet.

Glenville Tribune Newspaper (1996), 'Police actions under fire', 15 March.

Glenville Tribune Newspaper (1996), 'Bar owners win civil suit against city', 7 June.

Glenville Tribune Newspaper (1996), 'Police ready to review policies', 16 June.

Glenville Tribune Newspaper (1996), 'Glenville PD short of equality goal', 12 October.

Glenville Tribune Newspaper (1996), 'Glenville police officers seek union protection', 7 November.

Goldberg, David Theo (1993a), 'Modernity, Race and Morality', *Cultural Critique* (Spring).

Goldberg, David Theo (1993b), *Racist Culture: Philosophy and the Politics of Meaning*, Cambridge: Blackwell Publishers.

Goldstein, Herman (1977), *Policing a Free Society*, Cambridge, MA: Ballinger Publishing Company.

Hall, Stuart (1996), 'Introduction' in S. Hall and P. du Gay (eds), *Questions of Cultural Identity*, London: Sage.

Handberg, Roger (1980), 'Law, Coercion and Incentives: Reconciling the Irreconcilable', in John Brigham and Don W. Brown (eds), *Policy Implementation: Penalties or Incentives*, Beverly Hills, CA: Sage.

Handler, Joel (1986), *The Conditions of Discretion*, New York: Russell Sage Foundation.

Harding, Sandra (1987), 'The Curious Coincidence of Feminine and African American Moralities: Challenges for Feminist Theory', in E.F. Kittay and D.T. Meyers (eds), *Women and Moral Theory*, Totowa, NJ: Rowman & Littlefield.

Harding, Sandra (1990), 'Feminism, Science and the Anti-Enlightenment Critiques', in Linda J. Nicholson (ed.), *Feminism/Postmodernism*, New York: Routledge.

Harrington, Christine B. and Barbara Yngvesson (1990), 'Interpretive Sociological Research', *Law and Social Inquiry*, 15 (1).

Hartsock, Nancy (1990), 'Foucault on Power: A Theory for Women?', in Linda J. Nicholson (ed.), *Feminism/Postmodernism*, New York: Routledge.

Hepburn, E.R. (1993), 'Women and Ethics: A "Seeing" Justice?', *Journal of Moral Education*, 23 (1).

Herbert, Steve (1998), 'Police Subculture Reconsidered', *Criminology*, 36 (2).

Herbert, Steven (1997), *Policing Space: Territoriality and the Los Angeles Police Department*, Minneapolis: University of Minnesota Press.

Hogg, M.A. and D. Abrams (1988), *Social Identifications*, New York: Routledge.

Hummel, Ralph (1991), 'Stories Managers Tell: Why They are Valid as Science', *Public Administration Review*, 51 (1).

Huo, Yuen, Heather J. Smith and Tom R. Tyler (1996), 'Superordinate Identification, Subgroup Identification and Justice Concerns: Is Separatism the Problem; Is Assimilation the Answer?', *Psychological Science*, 7.

Institute for Law and Justice (1990), 'Organizational Analysis of the Glenville Police Department: A Report Submitted to the Glenville Police Department and City of Glenville', place of publication withheld to protect the confidentiality of the participants.

Jardine, Alice (1993), 'The Demise of Experience: Fiction as Stranger Than Truth?', in Thomas Docherty (ed.), *Postmodernism, A Reader*, New York: Columbia University Press.

Jones, Jacqueline (1992), *The Dispossessed: America's Underclasses from the Civil War to the Present*, New York: Basic Books.

Kerber, Linda K. (1986), 'Some Cautionary Words for Historians', *Signs*, 11 (2).

Kohlberg, Lawrence (1969), 'Stage and Sequence: The Cognitive-Developmental Approach to Socialization', in D.A. Goslin (ed.), *Handbook of Socialization Theory and Research*, Chicago: Rand McNally.

Krebs, Dennis L., Sandra C. Vermeulen, Kathy L. Denton and Jeremy I. Carpendale (1994), 'Gender and Perspective Differences in Moral Judgement and Moral Orientation', *Journal of Moral Education*, 23 (1).

Laclau, Ernesto and Lillian Zac (1994), 'Minding the Gap: The Subject of Politics', in Ernesto Laclau (ed.), *The Making of Political Identity*, London: Verso.

Leland, Suzanne and Steven Maynard-Moody (1998), 'Street-Level Discretion and Policy Implementation: The Multiple Principal Problem', paper presented at the Annual Midwest Political Science Association Meetings, Chicago, 23–5 April.

Lempert, Richard (1966), 'Strategies of Research in Legal Impact Studies', *Law and Society Review*, 1 (1).

Lipsky, Michael (1980), *Street-Level Bureaucracy: Dilemmas of the Individual in Public Services*, New York: Russell Sage Foundation.

Luria, Zella (1986), 'A Methodological Critique', *Signs*, 11 (2).

Lyons, William (1999), *The Politics of Community Policing: Rearranging the Power to Punish*, Ann Arbor: University of Michigan Press.

McGowan, Carl (1972), 'Rulemaking and the Police', *Michigan Law Review*, 70.

Manning, Peter (1977), *Police Work*, Cambridge, MA: MIT Press.

Manning, Peter (1989), 'Occupational Culture', in William Bailey (ed.), *Encyclopedia of Police Science*, New York: Garland.

Manning, Peter K. (1997), *Police Work: The Social Organization of Policing*, Prospect Heights, IL: Waveland Press.

Marenin, Otwin (1985), 'Police Performance and State Rule: Control and Autonomy in the Exercise of Coercion', *Comparative Politics*, 18 (1), October.

Maynard-Moody, Steven and Marisa Kelly (1993), 'Stories Public Managers Tell About Elected Officials: Making Sense of the Politics–Administration Dichotomy', in Barry Bozeman (ed.), *Public Management*, San Francisco: Jossey-Bass.

Maynard-Moody, Steven, Michael Musheno and Marisa Kelly (1995), 'Justice in the Delivery of Government Services: Decision Norms of Street-Level Bureaucrats', a grant proposal submitted to and awarded by the National Science Foundation.

Meyer, John C. (1995), 'Tell Me a Story: Eliciting Organizational Values from Narratives', *Communication Quarterly*, 43 (2), Spring.

Meyers, T. Kittay and Diana Eva Feder (eds) (1987), *Women and Moral Theory*, Totowa, NJ: Rowman & Littlefield.

Mies, Maria (1991), 'Women's Research or Feminist Research? The Debate Surrounding Feminist Research and Methodology', in Margaret Fonow and Judith A. Cook (eds), *Beyond Methodology: Feminist Scholarship as Lived Research*, Bloomington: Indiana University Press.

Mirande, Alfredo (1989), 'The Chicano and the Law: An Analysis of Community–Police Conflict in an Urban Barrio', in Harold Launer and Joseph Palenski (eds), *Crime and Immigrants*, Springfield, Illinois, USA: Charles C. Thomas.

Mouffe, Chantal (1995), 'Democratic Politics and the Question of Identity', in John Rajchman (ed.), *The Identity in Question*, New York: Routledge.

Mumby, Dennis K. (1987), 'The Political Function of Narrative in Organizations', *Communications Monographs*, 54.

Musheno, Michael (1986), 'The Justice Motive in the Social Policy Process: Searching for Normative Rules of Distribution', *Policy Studies Review*, 5 (4).

Musheno, Michael, Peter Gregware and Kriss Drass (1991), 'Court Management of AIDS Disputes: A Sociolegal Analysis', *Law and Social Inquiry*, 16.

Oberweis, Trish and Michael Musheno (1999), 'Policing Identities', *Law and Social Inquiry*, 24 (4).

Pleck, Elizabeth (1987), *Domestic Tyranny: The Making of American Social Policy against Family Violence from the Colonial Times to the Present*, New York: Oxford University Press.

Prottas, James (1979), *People-Processing*, Lexington, MA: Lexington Books.

Reuss-Ianni, Elizabeth (1983), *Two Cultures of Policing: Street Cops and Management Cops*, New Brunswick: Transaction Books.

Riessman, Catherine Kohler (1993), *Narrative Analysis*, Qualitative Research Methods Series, Vol. 30, Newbury Park: Sage.

Rosenwald, G.C. and R.L. Ochberg (1992), 'Introduction: Life Stories, Cultural Politics and Self-Understanding', in G.C. Rosenwald and R.L. Ochberg (eds), *Storied Lives: The Cultural Politics of Self-Understanding*, New Haven: Yale University Press.

Ross, Tom (1996), *Just Stories: How the Law Embodies Racism and Bias*, Boston: Beacon Press.

Russell, Diana E.H. (1982), *Rape in Marriage*, New York: Macmillan.

Samuels, Frederick (1977), *The Durable Group: Thoughts on Human Identity*, Washington, DC: The University Press of America.

Sarat, Austin (1985), 'Legal Effectiveness and Social Studies of Law: On the Unfortunate Persistence of a Research Tradition', *Legal Studies Forum*, 9 (1).

Sarris, Greg (1992), 'What I'm Talking About When I'm Talking About My Baskets: Interviews with Mabel McKay', in Sidonie Smith and Julia Watson (eds), *De/Colonizing the Subject: The Politics of Gender in Women's Autobiography*, Minneapolis: University of Minnesota Press.

Scott, Joan W. (1992), 'Experience', in Judith Butler and Joan W. Scott (eds), *Feminists Theorize the Political*, New York: Routledge.

Scott, Joan W. (1995), 'Multiculturalism and the Politics of Identity', in John Rajchman (ed.), *The Identity in Question*, New York: Routledge.

Sewell, William (1992), 'A Theory of Structure: Duality, Agency and Transformation', *American Journal of Sociology*, 98.

Shearing, Clifford D. and Richard V. Ericson (1991), 'Culture as Figurative Action', *British Journal of Sociology*, 42 (1).

Skogan, Wesley and Susan Hartnett (1997), *Community Policing, Chicago Style*, Oxford: Oxford University Press.

Smart, Carol (1989), *Feminism and the Power of Law*, London: Routledge.

State Republic Newspaper (1994), 'Glenville Chief Running for Jefferson City's Top Police Job', 10 August.

State Republic Newspaper (1994), 'Glenville's New Police Chief Returns to Old Beat', 14 December.

State Republic Newspaper (1995), 'Neighborless for now', 16 December.

State Republic Newspaper (1996), 'Glenville Cops Going Online to Fight Crime', 16 March.

State Republic Newspaper (1996), 'National Night Out! Join Crime Fight', 2 August.

State Republic Newspaper (1997), 'TV Becomes a Tool in Community Policing', 29 January.

State RSA (n.d.), 'Handbook for all Applicants and Individuals who are Eligible for RSA Services', unpublished office document.

State RSA (n.d.), unpublished informational document.

State RSA (n.d.), '[VR] Program Description', unpublished document.

Stiller, Nancy, J. and Linda Forrest (1990), 'An Extension of Gilligan and Lyon's Investigation of Morality: Gender Differences in College Students', *Journal of College Student Development*, 31.

Swidler, Ann (1968), 'Culture in Action: Symbols and Strategies', *American Sociological Review*, 51.

Tajfel, H. (1972), 'Social Categorization', English manuscript of 'La catégorisation sociale', in S. Moscovici (ed.), *Introduction à la Psychologie Sociale*, 1, Paris: Larousse.

Tajfel, H. (1978), 'Social Categorization, Social Identity and Social Comparison', in H. Tajfel (ed.), *Differentiation Between Social Groups: Studies in the Psychology of Intergroup Relations,* London: Academic Press.

Tetenbaum, Toby Jane and Judith Pearson (1989), 'The Voices of Children's Literature: The Impact of Gender on the Moral Decisions of Storybook Characters', *Sex Roles,* 20 (7/8).

Thoma, Stephen J. (1986), 'Estimating Gender Differences in the Comprehension and Preference of Moral Issues', *Developmental Review,* 6.

Trethewey, Angela (1997), 'Organizational Culture', in P.Y. Beyers (ed.), *Organizational Communication: Theory and Behavior,* Boston: Allyn and Bacon.

Trubek, David M. and John Esser (1989), '"Critical Empiricism" in American Legal Studies: Paradox, Program or Pandora's Box?', *Law and Social Inquiry,* 14.

Tushnet, Mark (1984), 'An Essay on Rights', *Texas Law Review,* 62 (8).

US Census Bureau (1990), Data for Monarch County, database C90STF3A.

Van Maanen, John (1978), 'The Asshole', in Peter Manning and John Van Maanen (eds), *Policing: A View From the Street,* Santa Monica, CA: Goodyear Publishing.

Vinzant, Janet and Lane Crothers (1996), 'Street-Level Leadership: Rethinking the Role of Public Servants in Contemporary Governance', *American Review of Public Administration,* 26 (4), December.

Vinzant, Janet and Lane Crothers (1998), *Street-Level Leadership: Discretion and Legitimacy in Front-Line Public Service,* Washington, DC: Georgetown University Press.

Walker, Lawrence (1984), 'Sex Differences in the Development of Moral Reasoning: A Critical Review', *Child Development,* 55.

Walzer, Michael (1983), *Spheres of Justice,* New York: Basic Books.

White, Hayden (1987), *The Content of the Form,* Baltimore: Johns Hopkins University Press.

Williams, Patricia J. (1991), *The Alchemy of Race and Rights: Diary of a Law Professor,* Cambridge, MA: Harvard University Press.

Yin, Robert (1977), 'Production Efficiency Versus Bureaucratic Self-Interest: Two Innovative Processes', *Policy Sciences,* 8.

Young, Iris Marion (1990), *Justice and the Politics of Difference,* Princeton, NJ: Princeton University Press.

Young, Robert (1981), 'Post-Structuralism: An Introduction', in Robert Young (ed.), *Untying the Text: a Post-Structuralist Reader,* Boston: Routlege & Kegan Paul.

Index